D1163920

ENAMELING
ON METAL

Enameling on Metal

Text:
Eva Pascual i Miró and the chapter titled "The History of Enameling on Metal" written by Núria López-Ribalta

Exercises:
Núria López-Ribalta, in collaboration with Rafael Arroyo, Montserrat Mainar, Gemma Moles, and Andreu Vilasís.

Photography:
Nos & Soto, Carme Carranza, the files of Núria López-Ribalta, and Bagues-Masriera Joiers (pages 17, 118, 122, 123, and 156)

Drawings:
Juame Farrés

First edition for the United States, its territories and possessions, and Canada published 2010 by Barron's Educational Series, Inc.

Original title of the book in Spanish:
El Esmalte
© Copyright Parramón Ediciones, S.A.,—World Rights
Published by Parramón Ediciones, S.A., Barcelona, Spain

Translated from Spanish by Michael Brunelle and Beatriz Cortabarria

English translation © 2010 by Barron's Educational Series, Inc.

All rights reserved.
No part of this publication may be reproduced or distributed in any form or by any means without the written permission of the copyright owner.

All inquiries should be addressed to:
Barron's Educational Series, Inc.
250 Wireless Boulevard
Hauppauge, New York 11788
www.barronseduc.com

ISBN-13: 978-0-7641-6297-8
ISBN-10: 0-7641-6297-7

Library of Congress Catalog Card. No.: 2009944059

Printed in China

9 8 7 6 5 4 3 2 1

Con

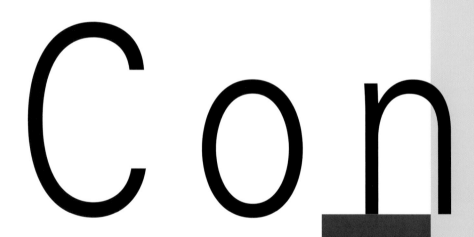

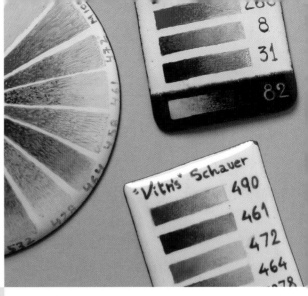

ents

Introduction

ired enamel on metal is an ancient art. Enamel is a type of glass specially formulated to be applied to metal. When it is fired in a kiln, enamel bonds closely to a substrate and covers its surface. The result is a very bright, glassy finish, with vibrant, durable colors, and the same qualities as glass. This artistic technique is also called vitreous enamel on metal, or simply enameling, which is the most common term. It is traditionally associated with sumptuous works of art like goldwork and jewelry, but it also has industrial applications. Today, it is known as an extremely versatile and expressive artistic technique. In the context of fine art, it has many interesting applications, including objects, jewelry, and murals. The finished pieces are very unique with a smooth, shiny surface not found in other art media.

The art of enameling on metal requires a good understanding of the materials that are used. Enamel artists are faced with a complex material whose special characteristics determine the final results, much like stained glass. Add to this the difficulties of working with metal substrates and parts, which are radically different from enamel in characteristics and behavior. It is important to completely understand both enamel and the metals as materials, as well as how they behave together during firing. Enameling demands technical rigor, from the preliminary steps (cleaning the metal and enamel, applying the enamel, and creating the palettes and tests), to the more advanced techniques; it is a constant learning process. However, it is a satisfying medium for the beginner because the results are very beautiful from the start, especially in terms of color and texture.

This book covers the basic techniques of the art of enameling on metal. The main techniques are explained in an understandable, yet thorough, way. The first of the book's five basic chapters gives a brief history of enameling. The next chapter is about enamel as a material, its forms and characteristics. After that, you'll find a complete explanation of all the materials and tools that are used with different enameling techniques. The fourth chapter, the longest, covers the technical processes that are involved, starting with the preliminary steps and moving on to the principal techniques. Finally, in the fifth chapter, the complete process is shown in a step-by-step format as well-known artists, who are recognized as masters of the medium, create five works of art.

This book does not attempt to be a definitive manual of enameling on metal; rather, it offers a clear and detailed look at the fundamentals of a demanding but gratifying discipline that requires constant studying. Strictly speaking, each technique deserves its own book, given the wide range of artistic possibilities enameling offers. Here, we offer a series of techniques that will be very useful in creating and experimenting, as well as ideas for developing new work in your own personal style. Enameling allows you to create work with very particular aesthetics, where the reflection of light and purity of the colors become the central elements of interest. This, combined with the unique qualities of enamel (such as shininess and smoothness), becomes the defining characteristic of the art form.

▲ Authors Núria López-Ribalta (right) and Eva Pascual (left) with photographer Joan Soto.

Núria López-Ribalta has a degree in Art History and a doctorate in Fine Arts from the University of Barcelona. She also graduated in Enameling from the Llotja School of Art and Design. A student and collaborator of Andreu Vilasís, she specializes in the history and techniques of enameling. She has been a professor at the Llotja School since 1978, where she became tenured in Drawing in 2008. She studied painting at the Real Círculo Artístico of Barcelona and at the Escola de Belles Arts Oficis d'Olot in Girona. She is conservator of the Museum of Contemporary Enamel Art (MECS) in Salou, Tarragona, and the president for Spain of the German company Creativ-Kreis International. She is a cofounder of the Center for Information and Diffusion of the Art of Enameling (CIDAE) and editor of its magazine, *L'Esmalt*. She has also written for many publications and given papers at international conferences and symposiums, and has organized enameling exhibitions and competitions. She has been a member of the jury of the International Biennial Of Enamel in Limoges, France, of the 2006 Tbîlisi Biennial in the Republic of Georgia, and of many competitions in Salou. She has her own enameling studio and regularly exhibits her drawings, paintings, and enamelwork.

In 1997 she received the Diploma Master Craftsman from the Catalonian government. She has participated in many individual and group shows in Japan, Canada, Germany, Great Britain, Italy, Belgium, Argentina, India, and the United States, and her work is part of the permanent collections of various museums in Russia, Hungary, France, Germany, the United States, and Spain, among others. She has received numerous international awards for her enamelwork, among them the 2005 Diploma of the Municipality at the International Biennial in Vilnius, Lithuania, and the 2001 Prize for Excellence at the 14th Cloisonné Jewelry Contest, the 2004 Prize for Quality Par Excellance at the International Enameling Art Exhibition, and the Prize for Integration of Materials at the 17th Cloisonné Jewelry Contest, the latter three held in Japan.

Eva Pascual i Miró has a degree in Art History from the University of Barcelona, and specialties in Museography, Design, and Restoration from the Polytechnic University of Catalonia and in Preventive Restoration from the Autonomous University of Catalonia. She has also studied marketing and administration for cultural businesses. Following a family tradition, she began learning about antiques at a young age, especially Catalonian furniture and medieval furniture, as well as medieval decorative arts, subjects on which she has written numerous articles. She has worked for several museums and cultural institutions in Catalonia, documenting collections of furniture and decorative arts, advocating for national treasures, and coordinating exhibitions. She has also worked for companies that offer services to cultural institutions. She has taught classes in history, documentation, and furniture restoration and often writes for the magazine *Estudi del Moble*. She is a coauthor of the books *Restoring Wood*, *Decorating Wood*, *Stained Glass*, and *Leather*.

*E*nameling on metal is an ancient art whose roots parallel human history. Having passed through periods of splendor and decadence, enameling today is completely alive and relevant, used not only for coloring metals in jewelry and goldworking but for common objects, architectural murals, and both sculpture and two-dimensional art. Enamel is fused to metal supports to impart to them a permanent finish with lively, durable, and practically inalterable colors. Countless pieces of enameled art have survived from as far back as the third millennium B.C.E., a testament to man's ability to adopt early glass technology and apply it to embellish metals with unique colors and textures. Knowing about the history of this ancient art makes it even more inspiring; the creativity and technical advances achieved by early people are surprising. The beauty of the objects shown in this book will also help you appreciate the art of enameling. Since ancient times, the creative human spirit has combined the richness of metals with the splendor of colored enamel to create the most beautiful of objects, which are now kept as treasures in cathedrals, monasteries, palaces, and museums the world over.

The History of
Enameling *on Metal*

The Art of Enameling on Metal

Origins

Vitreous enamel is a paste of crushed glass with the consistency of sand. It is applied to metal and then fired, which melts it and makes it adhere to the support. We can assume that its origin parallels the origin of glass, and its uses and technology, which date back to the third and fourth millennia B.C.E. and are attributed to the ancient Egyptians and Mesopotamians. Both civilizations developed technologies for glass and for goldworking with embedded glass pastes that can be considered the proto-enamels. The jewelry pieces they created combine areas of cloisonné made of semiprecious stones and glass paste, often carved, inserted, and inlaid between previously decorated leaves of gold. Among them, the treasures of Queen Pu-Abi of Tutankhamen, also known as Shubad (in the University of Pennsylvania, Baghdad, and British museums), circa 1500 B.C.E. (in the Egyptian Museum of Cairo) are good examples.

◄ On the previous page, Léonard Limosin (1505–1576-77). *Saint Michael Defeating the Dragon.* Grisaille on copper. Mid–sixteenth century. Musée Municipal de l'Evêché (Limoges, France).

▼ Royal scepter from the necropolis at Kourion. Mycenaean civilization. Cloisonné over gold. Eleventh century B.C.E. Archeological Museum of Nicosia (Cyprus).

◄ Bronze brooch. Rome. Carved enamel or champlevé. Galia (Vaison-la-Romaine). Third century. Musée des Antiquités Nationales (St. Germain-en-Laye, France).

▼ *Shield Offering of Battersea.* Celtic art (discovered in the Thames River near the port of Battersea, in London, United Kingdom). Gilded bronze and opaque red enamel. Metal Age, La Tène, Celtic Art. First century B.C.E. (350) 30⅝ × 8⅝ in (77.7 × 22 cm). British Museum (London). (Inv: P&EE 1857.7-15.1).

We use the term **proto-enamel** because it appears that the glass was not always applied and melted onto the metal in a single firing process. Instead, in some cases, the glass was poured in liquid form (by fusion) into the metal cavities, where it expanded, fitting perfectly into every nook and cranny and staying there after cooling.

Apparently, Phoenician sailors and travelers perfected and spread this glass technology and other related techniques, introducing them to the many colonies that they had established in that area all along the Mediterranean coast.

In his chronicles, Pliny the Elder recounts that this glass paste was discovered, by accident, when silica from the sand of the Mediterranean beaches fused with calcareous elements (shellfish) that adhered to the metal used for cooking and to stir the night fire.

The Ancient World

Metalworking in the Western world dates back to the year 2000 B.C.E.; however, the oldest traces of enamelwork found to date can be traced to the Mediterranean region, where pieces of gold jewelry enameled with the cloisonné technique were found in Mycenaean tombs on the island of Cyprus. These include a group of six rings from the late Bronze Age, dating to the thirteenth century B.C.E. found at the Kouklia site, and a royal scepter from the eleventh century B.C.E., which is better preserved, from the necropolis at Kourion. Both pieces are housed at the Museum of Nicosia. The glass paste was not inlaid but applied and melted directly over the gold. In classical Greece this technique was incorporated into jewelry (of which few samples remain) in the sixth century B.C.E. As a result of Phoenician influence, some pieces were discovered in the Mediterranean colonies, among them, a necklace from Cádiz (fifth and fourth centuries B.C.E.), and the "Tesoro del Carambolo" (Carambolo's Treasure) from Seville (pendant, eighth–sixth centuries B.C.E.), which was probably Phoenician, in the style of the indigenous Tartessian culture of the southern Iberian Peninsula. Rome left many more examples in Gallic France, some of which are preserved in the Metropolitan Museum of Art in New York City.

The Celtics and other nomadic groups that traveled through Europe left pieces made with a new inlay technique, found especially in Gallic sites, where a workshop and several enameling tools were also found (Musée des Antiquités Nationales de Saint Germain, in Laye, France). They are also credited with introducing enameling to the Western world. In history we often need to look at parallel origins rather than a single specific origin, as people often developed similar or identical technologies in different parts of the world with no apparent physical relationship. In the Eastern world, these techniques were also known, and they spread to Western countries through the constant invasions of the nomadic people coming from the Eurasian steppes. Among them were the Excites, a group that originated in Asia and that had advanced metal- and goldworking technologies typical of nomadic people that came into contact with the Greek world. During the Macedonian Era, the Greeks had expanded into the Crimean Peninsula, where there was a sort of international jewelry and goldworking shop and where enameling was well known and used in high-end, intricate pieces.

The attribution of the discovery of enameling on metal in the Western world to the Celtic culture is based on a famous text from the third century (circa 240 B.C.E.) by the Greek Philostratus, who lived in Rome. Referring to the Celts, Franks, Vikings, and Saxons, he recounts that the "barbarians from the North" melted some type of gray sand on metal, which upon cooling turned into a brightly colored, hard material. Certainly, these warrior people adorned their weapons, shields, horse harnesses, jewelry, and lucky charms with designs and decorative elements, filling hollowed areas of the metal with glass paste that melted in place at high temperatures. They invaded the Roman Empire and introduced this decorative technique in Central and Northern Europe. One such sample is the warrior treasure of Battersea (now in the British Museum in London), from the first century B.C.E.

At the same time that the Romans dominated the Mediterranean, in the first century B.C.E., important samples of enamel pieces turned up in the late Egyptian era that were attributed to the little-known Meroë culture from the Nubia region (the Treasure of the Queen Amanishakheto, 35–20 B.C.E.), which demonstrates the survival and evolution of these techniques in their places of origin.

The Middle Ages: From Cloisonné to Champlevé

During the Middle Ages, the Celtic culture continued to thrive in Northern Europe, especially in Ireland and on the British Isles where important discoveries like the seventh-century Treasure of Sutton Hoo have been made (British Museum).

In the East, the oldest origin for similar techniques is China. Therefore, from Egypt to China, or through Mediterranean influence, metal enameling reached the Byzantine Empire, which perfected it and where it reached its pinnacle, technically and artistically, in a world that had already been Christianized. The technique that was perfected was gold cloisonné. This accomplishment is disputed between the Republic of Georgia and Byzantium. The oldest traces of gold cloisonné in Georgia date back to the eighth century. The best examples are found in the Fine Arts Museum of Georgia (Tbilisi, Republic of Georgia): the *Martvili* Triptych and the *Khakhuli* Triptych from the ninth to the twelfth centuries. Gold cloisonné techniques were developed in the East until well into the Middle Ages in the form of icons and Georgia stretched their production into the fifteenth century. Among the best-known Byzantine examples is the *Pala d'Oro* (an altarpiece 131 × 83 inches [3.34 × 2.12 m]) in the Church of Saint Mark in Venice. A gilded silver work of a later period (Gothic style), it serves as the sumptuous background for the best Byzantine enamels (225 pieces, most of them from the twelfth century) that come

▶ *La Pala d'Oro*, detail of Saint Matthew. Gold, cloisonné enamel, and precious stones. Twelfth century. Basilica of Saint Mark (Venice, Italy).

from the Hagia Sophia of Constantinople. Other magnificent examples are housed in the National Museum in Budapest, Hungary: the crowns of Emperor Constantine Monomachus and Saint Stephen of Hungary (eleventh century). The museum also has one of the oldest examples of glass enameling in the tips of an old crown belonging to a Byzantine princess. Quite a few Byzantine pieces of gold enameled jewelry, which had great influence in the Western world after being exported to shops in Germany are preserved in Kiev, Ukraine and in Bulgaria.

After the fall of the Western Roman Empire, these improved techniques were introduced to a West that was more impoverished after the splendor of the classic Greco-Roman world, through political alliances with the Carolingian Empire and the Ottomans in Bizantium.

In the Middle Ages, Christianity extended throughout almost all of Europe. Metal techniques emerged and were perfected, and with them enamel, almost exclusively at the hands of monks and craftsmen working for the Church. Always related to religious subjects, objects to be sold for worship were produced in all of the artistic genres. Artistically, enameling had great influence in the northern Christian kingdoms. After eight centuries of Muslim occupation, only the kingdoms of Asturias and part of Catalonia in Spain escaped such influence. After Visigothic art, Asturian art has left us important pre-Romanic goldwork pieces—like the Cross of Victory, with cloisonné enamels (tenth century), in the Holy Chamber of Oviedo—that are closely related to Carolingian, Lombard, and Frankish art.

▲ Book of Gospels. Ottonian German shop. First quarter of the eleventh century (southwest Germany). Gold, precious stones, and gold cloisonné enameling on gold. 15½ × 12½ in overall (39.2 × 32 cm). Detail of Saint Luke the Apostle, Musée du Louvre (Paris, France) (O.A. cat. 13).

Medieval enameling techniques adapted quickly to the themes, forms, and economy of the new era. Therefore, gold cloisonné on gold gradually became the technique of **champlevé on copper**, later gilded. Precious metals were scant in the Western world, and it was impossible to compete with the luxury of the East. Copper, on the other hand, made work easier for Carolingians and Ottomans, who created important workshops, in the tenth–eleventh centuries. Their work evolved and was basically mass produced and marketed along the pilgrimage routes between the most important ecclesiastical sites. Among the first workshops were Merovingian abbeys (Conques) and Lombardian abbeys (Altar of Saint Ambrose in Milan and Iron Crown in Monza), where the transition from cloisonné to champlevé took place. But the most important center of production of the twelfth and thirteenth centuries and after was the city of **Limoges**, in central France, which supplied champlevé enameled pieces throughout the Middle Ages, including chests, reliquaries, crosiers, chalices, Eucharist doves, pyxes, crosses, vessels for incense, and all types of religious objects. The collections in the Musée de Cluny and the Louvre in Paris are worth mentioning. In the Limoges region, many churches house pieces on site like the chests of Ambazac, Bellac, and Saint Étienne de Gimel. Some of the themes on the chests are repeated, like the ones dedicated to Saint Valeria or Saint Thomas Becket. The funerary tombstones of Godofredo Plantagenet in Le Mans and in the Basilica of Saint Denis are also important.

The Iberian Peninsula soon figured out how to replicate this technique. The workshop in **Silos**, with its Arab Hispanic influence, flourished during the Romanesque era, and it extended its influence to France via the Camino de Santiago, to the point that some authors question not the influence of these workshops, but their Limousin origin.

In Spain, we find the only surviving great Romanesque enameled altarpieces from the twelfth century: in Santo Domingo de Silos,

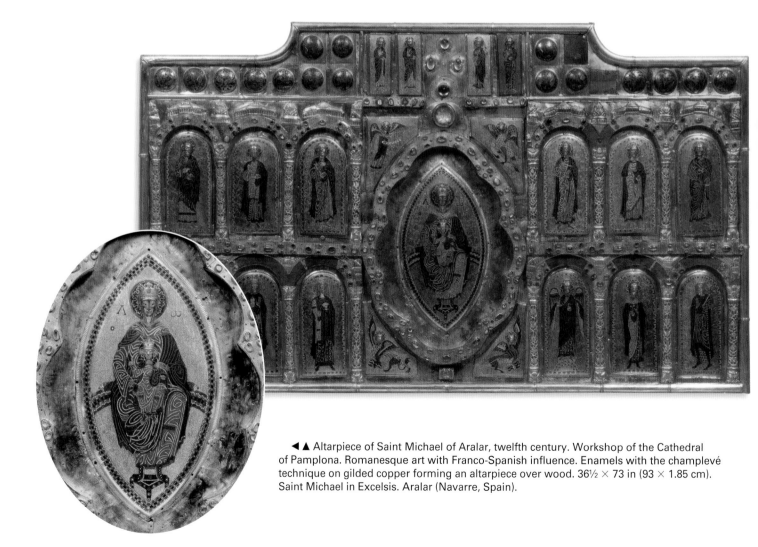

◀▲ Altarpiece of Saint Michael of Aralar, twelfth century. Workshop of the Cathedral of Pamplona. Romanesque art with Franco-Spanish influence. Enamels with the champlevé technique on gilded copper forming an altarpiece over wood. 36½ × 73 in (93 × 1.85 cm). Saint Michael in Excelsis. Aralar (Navarre, Spain).

Burgos, in Orense, and in Aralar, Navarre. Catalonia has only a few pieces; the most important is the *Misal de San Ruf* (Archives of the Chapterhouse of Tortosa) from the twelfth century, originating in northern of Catalonia.

Two other important centers—of greater artistic merit and technique but less known—were the **Meuse and the Rhine schools**. Among the pieces from the Rhine School are the Chest of the Magi, in the Cathedral of Cologne, and the Treasure of the Güelfos (twelfth century) by Master Eilbertus, in the Kunstgewerbe Museum in Berlin. Of the pieces from the Meuse School many were produced and/or preserved in present-day Belgium (Royal Museums of Fine Art in Belgium). The Tryptic of Stavelot is now in New York, and other pieces are in the British Museum. The only thing known about these medieval workshops is the name of the German monk Theophilus, who left a very important text: *Schedula Diversarum Artium*, the oldest technical text about metal and enameling technology.

At the end of the thirteenth century, among the Meuse and Rhine names we find Nicholas of Verdun, creator of part of the Chest of the Magi and of the altarpiece of Klosterneuburg, Austria, from 1811. After that, a new style began to emerge, the Gothic, which brought stylistic, conceptual, and technological changes.

The new idea that art should be light and that light leads to God emerged. With it the darkness of Romanesque art was forgotten, and artists let the light shine through Gothic stained glass windows. Therefore, Romanesque enamels (with specific exceptions in Venice, Byzantium, and Italy) were opaque. This was due to two technical reasons: the discovery of vitreous paste and coloring oxides, and copper, the base metal.

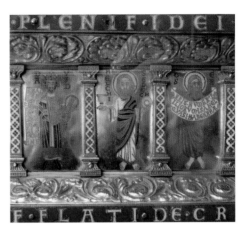

▲ Master Eilbertus. Portable altar, Cologne. 1150–1160. Enamel from the Meuse-Rhine Schools, with champlevé and cloisonné. Gilded copper over wood. 5⅛ × 11⅞ × 13¾ in (13 × 30 × 35 cm). Treasure of the Güelfos, Kunstgewerbe Museum (Berlin, Germany) (Inv. W. 11).

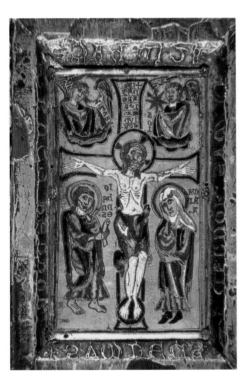

▲ Codex. *Misal de St. Ruf.* Romanesque art. Cover of the Book of Gospels, "Crucifixion." Champlevé enamel over copper, gilded. Molding/frame of the binding made of silver over wood. 10⁵⁄16 × 7¼ × 2¾ in (26.2 × 18.5 × 7 cm). Catalonian shop (Northern Catalonia. Avignon). Last third of the twelfth century. Archives of the Chapterhouse of Tortosa (Tarragona, Spain) (Inv. Ms. 11).

▶ *Chest of Saint Steven.* Copper and champlevé enamel, Limoges. Thirteenth century, between 1210 and 1220. National Museum of Art of Catalonia (Barcelona, Spain) (Inv. MNAC/MAC 65526.) Photo: Cabezas / Sagristá MNAC, 1995).

▲ Chalice of the Count of Mallorca. Gilded silver and transparent enamel in silver bas-relief. Barcelona, second half of the fourteenth century. 10 in high × 6¾ in (25 × 17 cm). Gothic style. Detail of the foot. Musée du Louvre (Paris, France). (O.A. Inv. 3359).

▼ *The Goldenes Rössel.* "Adoration of the Virgin Mary" reliquary. Paris, 1404. Gothic. Made for King Charles VI. Gold, ronde bosse enamel. 23 in high (58.4 cm). Housed in the collection of the Chapel of Altötting (Germany).

Transparent Enamels and the New Gothic Techniques

During the Gothic period, as cities and the bourgeoisie become more important, the economy allowed the Church to use silver, a precious metal that went well with the new transparent glass. Glass evolved, was perfected, and, thanks to research by master glassmakers, the color palette grew to include cobalt blues, bright reds, and emerald greens. Glassmakers, goldsmiths, and enamel artists mingled in cities and cathedrals. Thus, enamel artists began to apply to silver the same more perfect, transparent glass used in the stained glass windows that adorned the cathedrals. A metalworker of the fourteenth century who carved the copper champlevé learned to perfect his carvings and make them more detailed, almost drawing-like. Metalworkers practiced repoussé as well and not only alternated metal and enamel but completely covered the metal with transparent enamels, allowing the drawing to remain visible.

The **basse-taille** technique emerged. Unpredictably, the artistic dominance of Limoges declined and Italy reclaimed it, with the Siena shops producing the best work. For historic and political reasons, Catalonia joined in the production of enamels with all the luxurious detail of the period, becoming the second center of importance. The Cathedral of Girona, with its main altar and its diocesan museum, is proof of this. The shops in Mallorca produced high-end chalices and crosses. The Louvre Museum owns a few purely Catalonian ones, dating back to the fifteenth century. Paris also contributed important pieces from the magnificent Burgundian court of the 1400s, with

exceptional pieces in the technique called ***ronde bosse*** on gold. The *Goldenes Rössel* (Paris, 1404) which is now housed in the Chapel of Altötting (Germany), is a display of the technique and refinement of these enameled pieces. The French also contributed the small mirrors of Louis of Anjou (Musée du Louvre) of 1379, made in basse-taille on gold, and the famous Royal Gold Cup (end of the fourteenth century, British Museum, London), with its agitated history. The pictorial use of transparent enamels, the figures, and the general artistic evolution led the transition to the "painted enamels" of the Renaissance.

Independence from Metalworking: The Birth of Painted Enamel

The Renaissance marks a very important departure in the history of enamel art. Until then, enamel was subordinate to fine art and connected to the world of metalworking or to jewelry, as a complementary technique. Enamel did not exist as a separate craft. With the beginning of the Renaissance, enamel artists became independent. They decided that they could create and use enamel as a pictorial technique that stood on its own. New materials were favorable to this move.

All this formed part of the evolution of art in general. The Renaissance was a period of human development and a flowering of artistic capabilities. Detaching themselves from religion, artists felt free, and at the center of the universe. Techniques like printmaking emerged, allowing the popularization of art. Cultural exchanges became easier, and images crossed borders with greater speed.

In northern Italy, there was a clumsy, but successful, transition from basse-taille to painted enamel. Venetian painted enamels are proof of this. Limoges once more emerged from the ashes on its own merit. There, workshops that had maintained their technical knowledge resurfaced with completely new aesthetics, making prints of paintings. The subjects were religious at first, but little by little pagan and mythological themes emerged. During the fifteenth–seventeenth centuries, all of Europe was prolific in producing triptychs, polyptychs, and polychromatic plaques made by juxtaposing and superimposing colors without metal separations, free of silver and gold adornments. Toward the 1530s, the **grisaille** technique emerged, which gave way to monochromatic enamels, a result of copying prints (see

◄ Léonard Limosin. *Venus and Love.* Enamel painted on copper. Limoges, sixteenth century. Renaissance (France), 1555. 7½ × 10¼ in (19 × 26 cm). Musée du Louvre (Paris, France) (Inv. MR R274) (autre inv. N1251).

▼ Pierre Courteys (d. 1580). *Laocoön,* c.1559. Painted polychrome enamel on copper. Musée Municipal de l'Evêché (Limoges, France).

image on page 9). The best specialists were in the workshops of Limoges. Their research produced a semitranslucent white enamel that allowed them to model the anatomy of the body in chiaroscuro, in a pictorial manner that did not exist until then. It is known as "Limoges white" in tribute to its origin. The grisaille technique was perpetuated for two-and-a-half centuries, and was combined with painted enamels on copper plaques and objects like water stands, china, boxes, candelabra, trivets, and the like. Among the notable artists, the following family names stand out: Reymond, Penicaud, Limosin, Court (including a woman, Suzanne Court), Courteys, and Nouailher. Some works were anonymous, signed *Maître aux grand fronts* or *Maître de l'Énéide*, as enamel painting always imitated studio painting. Thanks to his creations, Léonard Limosin reached the status of royal painter. The Musée Municipal de l'Evêché in Limoges has a magnificent collection of grisaille and painted enamels from the Renaissance and Baroque periods. The Musée du Louvre houses the most spectacular pieces by Léonard Limosin, a portrait of Grand Master Anne de Montmorency (1556) and two altarpieces depicting the Crucifixion and the Ascension, among others. It also has an exceptional collection of painted enamels and grisaille pieces from the sixteenth and seventeenth centuries.

However, applied enamel (jewelry and gold pieces) does not disappear completely in the Renaissance. There are examples of plique-à-jour enamels with cloisonné and

▲ Léonard Limosin. *Portrait of the Future François II.* Enamel painted on copper. 17⅜ × 12¼ in (44 × 31 cm). Renaissance. Musée du Louvre (Paris, France) (Inv. N1253).

ronde bosse, in Parisian and German Gothic style, and these techniques continued into the Baroque and Rococo periods, along with other techniques that will be covered later. The famous sculptor and goldsmith Benvenuto Cellini sculpted and enameled an exceptional piece in 1543: *Gold Salt Cellar for King Francis I* (Kunsthistorisches Museum, Vienna, Austria). He also left a treatise on silver- and goldworking that includes enamelwork of invaluable historic relevance. (See the Bibliography.)

▲ Enameled piece of jewelry from the late Renaissance period. Spain. Seventeenth century. Ronde bosse enamel on gold. National Museum of Decorative Arts (Madrid, Spain) (Inv. CE1869).

Public boredom and changing trends prompted a reduction in the number of workshops as well as a decrease in clientele. As a result, the quality of the pieces suffered and technical perfection was lost, giving rise to a major decline that, aggravated by the plague, almost obliterated the craft in the last third of the seventeenth century. The Nouailher and Laudin families were the last ones to continue to practice the craft during this period, but they abandoned perfection and transparencies and devoted themselves instead to painting small objects and religious plaques on white backgrounds; ultimately, they copied motifs with a commercial, not an artistic, end. This new technique became known as **painting on enamel**. It was born in France, in the Loire area (the workshops of Blois) in the mid-seventeenth century, and it was perfected in England, which saved the craft. In the seventeenth century it reached its pinnacle in Geneva, Switzerland, the main center of production, expansion, and virtuosity. In reality, this became a sub-technique of the previous one, painted polychrome enamels, which was used in combination with other techniques for details, texts, and so on. It is a very appropriate pictorial technique for **miniatures**, which involves applying metal oxides on previously enameled surfaces. The new Rococo taste for playful, luxurious, collectable objects

provided an opportunity to hone this technique until it reached perfection.

Miniatures—portraits primarily, followed by mythological themes, courtiers, frivolous subjects for small boxes, and expensive pocket watches—restore the splendor of enameling art with this new fashion. Worth mentioning among the French imitators of the art are Jean and Henri Toutin and the Huaud brothers, some of whom emigrated to Geneva. From the miniature school in Geneva, the painters Liotard, Thouron, Soiron, and Glardon stand out. In addition, an endless array of refined *objets de vertu* were enameled on precious metals with backgrounds elaborated with the *guilloché* technique that survived during the nineteenth century in Geneva, Paris, and England. The best collections can be found in the Musée International d'Horlogerie in La Chaux-de-Fonds, Switzerland, as well as in the Museum of Decorative Arts in Barcelona.

At the same time, a unique silver- and gold-working hub was developing in the Central European court of the Hapsburgs, in the Nuremberg workshops, which reached surprising technical levels in the technique of ronde bosse. Examples include *Palace of the Great Mongol* (1701–1708) by Johann Melchior Dinglinger, which is preserved in the Grünes Gewölbe (Dresden, Germany), and the royal collections of Munich and Copenhagen.

However, at the end of the eighteenth century, the excessive proliferation of objects and *chinoiserie* resulted in vulgarization and boredom, which caused a progressive decline that extended through most of the nineteenth century, until enameling was almost completely forgotten.

▼ Christofle. Paris / St. Denis. Nineteenth century. *Yellow Irises* vase. Paris, Reiber design, 1874. Foundry cloisonné. Gilded bronze. Musée Bouilhet-Christofle (St. Denis, France) (ref: G950).

▲ Watch with enamel miniature. *Offering*. Painting over enamel on gold and *guilloché* background with blue transparent enamel. End of the eighteenth century. 2 in diameter (5 cm). Directoire. Gold and pearls. Geneva (Switzerland). Watch brand: Monnier et Mussard. Museum of Decorative Arts, Barcelona (Spain) (Inv. 38790).

Industrialization and New Possibilities: From the Recovery of Ancient Techniques to the Splendor of Art Nouveau and Art Deco

In the last third of the nineteenth century, the various enameling techniques were revived thanks to the interest of antique dealers and archeologists.

At the same time, enamel on iron was developed as a novelty for the incipient industry, for utilitarian objects, and especially for advertising and road signs, which greatly influenced subsequent development of artistic enamelwork in the twentieth century and continue to do so today, providing new possibilities for architectural siding, interior murals, industrial design, urban sculpture, and more. France (specifically Morez) and Germany stand out in this area.

The Nineteenth Century

Besides the Industrial Revolution, there were other circumstances that caused the recovery. Antique dealers and jewelers, during the artistic revival phase, pushed the craftsmen toward recovery. The first technical manuals were written in France; Paris and Sèvres were the center of the revival. Famous names included Wagner, Froment-Meurice, Falize, Boucheron, Christofle, Tard, Barbedienne (enamel on goldwork), and Grandhomme, Garnier, Popelin, Lepec, A. Meyer, and the Soyers (painted enamel). The Manufacture of Sèvres, specializing in porcelain

▲ Théophile Soyer (Paris, 1853–1940). Grisaille on copper. Revival style from the nineteenth century (in the manner of Limoges). Paris, 1889. 7¼ × 4⅛ in (18.5 × 10.5 cm). Private collection of Lilian Menache, Mexico.

◄ Lluís Masriera (1872–1958). Brooch. Barcelona, c. 1902. Modernism. *Winged Nymph.* 2¾ × 2½ in (7 × 6.5 cm). Gold, opals, pearl, and diamonds. Ronde bosse on repoussé and plique-à-jour. Bagués-Masriera Collection (Marseille, Spain).

► Lluís Masriera (1872–1958). Brooch. Barcelona, c. 1912. Pendant. *Landscape.* 2⅛ × 1½ in (5.5 × 3.7 cm). Yellow gold, diamonds, pearls, rubies, and plique-à-jour. Bagués-Masriera (Barcelona, Spain).

◄ Eugène Feuillâtre (1870–1916). Box. *Bats.* Paris,1900. Art Nouveau. Silver on enameled basse-taille with opaline tones and cloisonné. Kunstgewerbe Museum (Berlin, Germany).

and ceramic pieces, created a research center for materials and techniques that included, between 1845 and 1872, a shop for enamels on metal from which many interesting works of art and good techniques and artists emerged. Some of these artists (Meyer-Heine, Gobert, De Courcy, Philip, the Apoils, and Robillard) formed a very important nineteenth-century "neo"-style generation, without which enamel would not exist today. In Limoges only J. B. Ernest René Ruben and Dalpayrat worked with enamel, along with Delphine de Cool, who succeeded later in Paris as a grisaille expert and teacher, and later Blancher and Bourdery.

The spread of enamel and its appreciation can be attributed to large international expositions. Its enormous popularity was also a result of the new popular style, stimulated by the English Arts and Crafts movement and Art Nouveau, which, from the last decades of the nineteenth century and until 1910, positioned themselves at the forefront of European art. This style homogenized all the arts, and all the places they were made, while setting them apart at the same time. Enamel jewelry gained an unimaginable popularity that continues to this day. René Lalique, Thesmar, Fouquet, Vever with Tourette and Grasset, Feuillâtre, Gaillard, Wolfers, von Cranach, Christofle, and Lluís Masriera are key European names, as is Tiffany in the United States.

Among all the top techniques revived (grisaille, painted enamel) and other revitalized ones (industrial champlevé, cloisonné, faux cloisonné), **plique-à-jour** became very popular. Most of the modernist, naturalist, and Japanese-influenced jewelry was decorated with this technique. Meanwhile, following the adoption of opalescent and translucent enamels, transparencies decorated the wings of insects and fantasy characters everywhere. They were also used to cover small figures made of gold with the ronde basse technique, in matte or glossy finishes, reinstating the Parisian and Renaissance Gothic technique and the German Baroque that had been popular years earlier.

▲ Decorative spoon. Russia or Scandinavia. End of nineteenth to early twentieth century. Glass enamel in silver filigree. 7 in (18 cm). Attributed to the Ovchinnikov workshops, Saint Petersburg / Moscow, or imitators. Private collection (Barcelona, Spain).

Other variations surfaced as well: enamel over machine-carved metal, and guilloche—which Christofle and Fabergé, and later Cartier, popularized—in a modern variation of enameled basse-taille. Russia adhered to Art Nouveau through Fabergé, as a result of French influence, and it also perpetuated the painting over enamel technique of which it had produced important craftsmen in the eighteenth century. Machine production incorporated transferred images and serigraphy in the works of the nineteenth and twentieth centuries for commercial and artisanal, as well as artistic purposes, especially in England (Battersea and later Bilston).

The place of the technique was solidified thanks to the creation of art and craft schools during the eighteenth century and to enameling's overall growth during the twentieth century. Alexander Fisher, the author of an enameling manual, was an important figure in England, and in Geneva, the followers of Lossier, like Le Grand Roy, Dufaux, Henri Demole, and B. Schmidt-Allard, the last teacher from Geneva, to whom we owe the art's continuity in Catalonia—and, in fact, in all of Spain—because it is in Barcelona where the craft was preserved after being lost in the rest of the Peninsula. Craftsmen from Spain like Masriera, Pelegrí, and V. Corberó went to Geneva to learn the craft.

The Twentieth Century

L. Hirtz, Paul Grandhomme with Alfred Garnier, The Genevans Autran, Piguet, Millenet, and Meroz-Lossier, and artists from Limoges like Paul Bonnaud, and Jules and Robert Sarlandie introduced enamel to Art Nouveau with the reproduction of works by renowned artists like Mucha and the Symbolists. They also introduced large objects like vases, lamps, and plates, forcing the new generations from Limoges to slowly revitalize their *savoir faire* of the past. Finally, artists like Alexandre Marty and his daughter Henriette, Camille Fauré, and Leon Jouhaud emerged from Limoges, putting this area back on the international map during the Art Deco period of the 1920s and 1930s. Vases from the Fauré workshop are now considered very valuable art pieces and are sought after by collectors; recently they have also been the subjects of publications and retrospective exhibits. In Germany, at the Burg Giebichenstein Art School (1915–1933), closely connected to Bauhaus, professors like Maria Likartz and Lili Schultz, who were active in the periods between the wars, formed the foundation of the present-day generation of German enamel artists. Names like J. Goulden, R. Barriot (France), and De Poli (Italy) complete this group.

In Spain, Miquel Soldevila and others from the Escuela Massana, following the technique of Garnier and Grandhomme, formed a group of creative enamel artists that continued in the tradition of the painted enamel movement known as the "Escuela de Barcelona," whose name derives from modernist enamels

▼ Camille Fauré workshop (1872–1955). Limoges (France), 1925. Art Deco-style vase. Relief painted enamel on copper (recovered with silver foil). Kunstgewerbe Museum (Berlin, Germany).

▼ Josep Brunet (1911–1997). *Repòs 1.* Miniature enamel painted over copper. Barcelona School, 1986. 4 × 2½ in (10 × 6.5 cm). Private collection (Barcelona, Spain).

▲ Miquel Soldevila (1886–1956). *Maternitat*. Barcelona School. 1945. Pendant. Miniature enamel painted over copper (paint over enamel). Original gold frame 1⅜ × 1 in (3.5 × 2.5 cm). Private collection (Barcelona, Spain).

by Lluís Masriera, especially his "enamel cameos," in which he applied stained glass technique to modernist jewelry. From 1950 to 1960 the names Josep Brunet, Núria Nialet, Francesca Ribas, Núria Ribot, and Joan Gironès stand out.

The characteristics of this school can be seen in the work of internationally renowned enamel artists like F. Vilasís-Capalleja, Montserrat Mainar, Pascual Fort, and Andreu Vilasís, director and professor of the Llotja School of Barcelona. From the 1970s up to the new millennium, their work promoted a revival of enamel in Spain, in the same way that Professor Walter Lochmüller and the Pforzheim and Hanau schools did in Germany.

Centers of learning like the Bauhaus allowed Germany and Spain (Catalonia), and to some degree also Great Britain, to produce the best enamel artists of the twentieth century. Interestingly, France, once the leader of this art, saw it decline as a result of lack of teaching until Georges Magadoux created the International Biennials of Enamel Art in 1971, active until 1994. These gatherings were an impressive stimulus for the evolution and recognition of enamel as the highest form of art.

Contemporary Art, Design, and Jewelry

In France, especially in Limousin, some isolated names rather than groups emerge; this is due to a closed system for passing down knowledge. R. Restoueix, the brothers Betourné, and the Chéron family are among the traditional figures; among the reformists, Christian Christel, Roger Duban, B. Veisbrot, H. Martial, M. T. Masias, and J. C. Bessette are at the forefront of the French artists of the last century. Currently, Dominique Gilbert and the Galérie du Canal group are revitalizing the art together with other young artists in other European centers. Among the Germans are Herbert Martius, I. Martin, H. Blaich, U. Zehetbauer, M. Duntze, S. A. Klopsch, and E. Massow; in Great Britain, the group Fusion Studio of London and B.S.O.E.; in the Netherlands, Go de Kroon, Adriaan Van den Berk, and Han de Valk; the Japanese, in the style of cloisonné "shippo" objects, professors Kioko Iio, Hoshiko Yokoyama, Nobuko Horigome, Yokho Yoshimura, and Ohta, together with the murals of Toshiko and Mamoru Tanaka; and finally the American Stefan Knapp. Worth mentioning also are the Americans M. Seeler, K. Whitcomb, K. F. Bates, J. Schwarcz, and J. Tanzer, and the Russians, Georgians, and Hungarians who worked in the Kecskémet workshop and who continue to get together at current international gatherings. Biennial exhibitions that are no longer held in Limoges are now emerging elsewhere, like the "El Món de l'Esmalt" in Salou, Catalonia (Spain), the "Rencontres" in Morez, France, or the two international Japanese exhibitions in Tokyo. A competition was held in Coburg, Germany, until 1995, and in Keckskémet, Hungary, a pioneering international symposium (since 1979). There are also several contests in Austria and the United States, notably the ones organized by the Enamelist Society and the Carpenter Foundation. Other initiatives are being pursued in Eastern European countries (Lithuania, Georgia, Russia).

It is important to mention the emergence of thematic museums, including the pioneering effort of the MECS in Salou, Catalonia (Spain), followed by others in Himmerod (Germany), Syosenkyo Ropeway Shippo in Japan, the W. W. Carpenter Foundation in the United States, Ravenstein (Holland), and Blieskastel (Germany). Permanent collections exist in Villa Vertua, Milan (Italy), and Kecskémet (Hungary), and open contemporary enamel workshops in Erfurt (Germany), Budafok (Hungary), and Palanga and Klaipeda (Lithuania).

Important worldwide art museums like the Louvre and the Arts Décoratifs (both in Paris), the Metropolitan Museum (New York), the Kunstgewerbe (Berlin), the Angewandte Kunst (Cologne), MNAC (Barcelona), Evêché (Limoges), the British Museum, and the Victoria and Albert (both in London) are giving more importance and devoting more space to collections of enamel objects.

All of these efforts have positioned twenty-first-century enamel as a discipline in all the fields of plastic expression. They also have favored a growing use of design objects and contemporary jewelry, whose infinite possibilities are constantly being renewed thanks to new generations of young people who are fond of it and to enthusiastic admirers.

▶ Andreu Vilasís (Barcelona, 1934). *Jardí*. Enamel painted over copper. 8⅝ × 13 in (22 × 33 cm). Barcelona, 2006. Original wood frame and support by the artist himself. Private collection. (Barcelona, Spain).

*B*efore studying the necessary materials and tools, it is important to be familiar with the characteristics of enamel and the different techniques employed in enamelwork. Enamel, as a vitreous paste, has all the same characteristics as glass. First, it's essential to understand the particular nature of glass and its physical and chemical characteristics, as well as the process of making the enamel that you will use in the studio. We must also examine the nature of enamel—which is essentially a special kind of glass formulated to be applied to metal—to determine its qualities and behavior. Knowledge of enamel as a material is critical to the success of your future enamelwork.

In this chapter, we introduce the different kinds of enamel and the forms in which they come to us from the manufacturers, ready for use in the studio. We will also explain the characteristics of enamel and its behavior during firing, giving you an idea of what is necessary to create successful work.

Enamel

Enamel as a Material

Enamel is a special kind of glass formulated specifically to be applied to metal, to which it bonds closely and covers when fired in a kiln. Its basic ingredients are similar to those of normal glass; its composition is most similar to that of a certain variety of glass known as crystal. Like crystal, enamel has, among other unique characteristics, a softening temperature lower than that of other glasses, at which it flows and melts to bond to the metal.

Physical and Chemical Characteristics

Enamel, and by extension all glass, has a particular chemical makeup that accounts for its plastic qualities and behavior. Although glass appears to be solid, chemically speaking it is a super-cooled liquid. This concept is not difficult to understand if we consider the idea of structure and the states of matter: solid, liquid, and gas. Matter is formed by atoms that join to become molecules, which in turn join with each other in reaction to forces that create specific structures. Glass has an amorphous structure—that is, indefinite or irregular—a characteristic that makes it more like liquids than crystals. The molecules of liquids do not have fixed positions but continually move around. They do not have a form of their own; they adapt to the container they are in. The crystalline structure of solids is owing to atoms and molecules that are arranged in specific, repeating patterns. They occupy fixed positions, and they only move by vibrating around a point. This repeated pattern is not present in glass, whose atoms and molecules are fixed in a disorganized arrangement from the time the glass solidifies at the end of the manufacturing process; in other words, they have an amorphous structure similar to that of liquids. However, in liquids the atoms and molecules move freely, while those in glass stay in fixed positions. After glass is created by melting its different components, it is cooled until it hardens without passing through a crystallization stage, resulting in a vitreous state. This trait of glass defines its behavior and properties (it is a hard solid but very fragile, for example), and its characteristic transparency and sheen.

Components and Manufacture

Components

Enamel, like all glass, is a material made from several different ingredients: silica (the basic ingredient of glass), flux, stabilizers, and secondary materials like colorants and ingredients to make it opaque.

Silica, in the form of silica dioxide or S_iO_2, which can be siliceous sand or vitrified in its natural forms of quartz or rock crystal, is the basic component of enamel. Because silica becomes fluid at very high temperatures, around 3,000°F (1,700°C), it is necessary to add other ingredients (flux) to lower the temperature. By itself, silica would make an easily shattered, fragile material that would be impossible to work with, so it is also necessary to add components to harden it (stabilizers). The fusion and subsequent cooling of the silica results in an amorphous material that has the same chemical composition but with a crystalline structure whose layers of atoms and molecules disperse the light. The silica, lacking a concrete structure like that of quartz, becomes a transparent material that allows light to pass through.

Fluxes help the silica melt by lowering its temperature. Sodium carbonate (Na_2CO_3, commonly called soda ash or soda crystals), sodium borate ($Na_2B_4O_7 \cdot 10H_2O$, known as borax), potassium hydroxide (KOH, also known as potash), and others are used. Stabilizers add hardness and body to the material and make it non-soluble; without these ingredients, it would even be water-soluble. Lead oxide (PbO) or lead tetroxide (Pb_3O_4, or $2PbO \cdot PbO_2$), also called minium or red lead because of its color, are added at the end to give the material density and sheen and add the malleability required for working.

Enamels have some characteristics in common with crystal, a kind of high-quality glass with unique properties. Other compounds, mainly metal oxides, are added to create color, in a proportion that varies from 2 to 15% depending on the glass that is used. However, coloring is a complex process encompassing many variables: the behavior of each kind of glass, the effects of reduction or oxidation caused by the firing, the chemical composition of each product or coloring agent, the fusion temperature of the kiln, and the duration of the process. It is possible for a single compound to make different colors depending on the temperature reached during the manufacture of the glass, for example. Other components, like tin oxide (SnO) and antimony trioxide (Sb_2O_3), among others, are used to make the materials opaque; the enamel can be made more opaque or opalescent according to the proportions of the mix.

▲ Quartz.

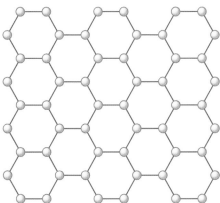

▲ A model of the atomic structure of an ordered material (crystal).

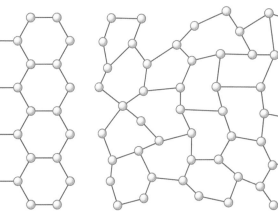

▲ A model of the atomic structure of an amorphous material (glass).

▲ Minium.

Manufacture

Today, enamels are manufactured in very specialized factories with sophisticated equipment. They are made with very specific processes that require exact proportions of each ingredient. First, the required amounts of each ingredient are placed in a crucible. Crucibles are made by hand of refractory ceramic, which is highly resistant to heat, and allowed to dry for at least seven months at about 86°F (30°C) before they are used. To make the enamel, the crucible is gradually heated in the kiln for eight days until it reaches the desired temperature (usually about 2,550°F [1,400°C]). Then the compo-

nents of the enamel are poured into it. In the first phase, as the components melt, a transparent, uncolored base enamel called flux or frit is created, which is used as the raw material for the finished enamel in the second melting. The color agents are added to this frit; different mixes and compositions are used to create the desired colors. The mixture is placed in the crucible and put in the kiln at 2,550°F (1,400°C) for about fourteen hours for 440 pounds (200 k) of material. At the end of this time, a fluid mass with a pasty consistency is obtained. It is removed from the crucible using large cups with long handles and poured onto metal tables, where it is allowed to cool slowly until it solidifies. The result is a flat, circular sheet. (It is also possible to pour the mass into a mold to create a dalle, a solid rectangular block, or directly into water to make granules). Then the sheets are broken up and ground in special mills containing balls made of porcelain (or, more recently, extremely hard synthetic resin), to make rather fine grains. During the grinding, it is important to avoid mixing colors, and the resulting granules should be as regular as possible. Next, the enamel goes through different processes to eliminate dust (with fans) and possible metallic particles (with electromagnets). Finally, the material is separated according to the size of the particles using sieves with different sizes of mesh screens.

▲ Enamel is made from several materials. Silica is the basic ingredient.

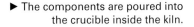

► The components are poured into the crucible inside the kiln.

◄◄ When the molten enamel is ready, it is removed from the crucible with a long-handled cup and poured on metal tables, where it cools.

◄ Once the disks have hardened, they are removed with a spatula, deposited in metal boxes, and broken with a metal bar. Then they are mechanically ground.

▲ Pieces of a transparent enamel disk before it is ground.

◄ Transparent enamel dalle with a molded reference mark.

▼ Crucibles used for making samples of different enamels in small amounts.

COMMON COLORANTS	
Product	**Color**
Copper oxide	Green tones
Cobalt oxide	Blue tones
Manganese oxide	Violet tones
Gold compounds and copper oxide	Red tones
Platinum oxide	Light gray tones
Cadmium sulfate	Yellow tones
Iridium oxide	Black tones
Iron oxide	Brown tones

Coloring glass during its fabrication is a highly complex process with many physical and chemical variables. Besides the coloring agents, many other factors come into play: the composition of the glass, the temperature, the kind of kiln, and so on. The proportion of the colorants and the possible mixtures of the coloring agents also play a large part.

The different kinds of enamel are classified by the way they look after firing and how they react to light, as well as by their composition (if they contain lead or not) and their manufacturer. They can also be classified by how they react to temperature—that is, the range at which they become fluid and bond with the metal (see page 60).

Transparent Enamels

Flux

Flux is a transparent enamel that is considered separately because of its characteristics and use. It is transparent and colorless, and is mainly used as a preparatory layer or covering for metals before the enamel is applied to them. It protects the support by keeping oxygen away from the metal and acts as an insulating layer between it and the enamel, which is very important when working with transparent enamels. It is also used as a preparatory layer for bonding some elements (pieces of gold or silver, for example), and as a final covering layer for vitrifiable paint and decals, to even out the surface of the work. There are specific fluxes for each metal—copper, silver, and gold are primarily used—and for finishes. Some manufacturers make fluxes specifically as coatings that create a very glossy finish over enamelwork and protect vitreous paint.

▲ Flux for copper.

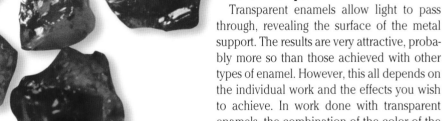

▶ A piece of copper with a baked-on layer of flux.

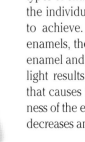

▶ Lumps of transparent enamel.

Other Transparent Enamels

Transparent enamels allow light to pass through, revealing the surface of the metal support. The results are very attractive, probably more so than those achieved with other types of enamel. However, this all depends on the individual work and the effects you wish to achieve. In work done with transparent enamels, the combination of the color of the enamel and the metal surface that reflects the light results in a very interesting luminosity that causes the coloring to vary. As the thickness of the enamel increases, the transparency decreases and the color is intensified.

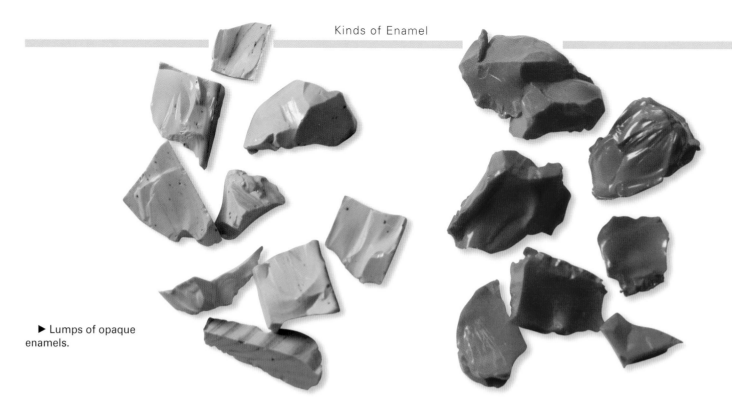

► Lumps of opaque enamels.

Silver and gold metal supports create interesting results because of their reflective qualities. Enamel usually can be applied directly to the metal, but blue and gray enamels tend to look green and turquoise because the yellow reflections of the gold mix with the colors. To counteract this effect, a layer of a special flux is applied to the gold and fired before adding colored enamels. A layer of flux is also applied to silver to avoid direct contact between the metal and yellow-, orange-, and red-toned enamels; otherwise, chemical changes during firing affect the enamel's color and transparency.

When it comes to copper, a layer of flux can be applied first, or the enamel can be applied directly to the metal. Yellows, blues, and violets are especially good for this, although it depends on the characteristics of each enamel and its manufacturer. Transparent enamels allow for the creation of very interesting effects on textured, engraved, and carved surfaces. They are used primarily for painted enamel, stained glass, cloisonné, and basse-taille. They are available in a wider color range than the rest of the enamels.

Opaque Enamels

Opaque enamels do not allow light to pass through, hiding the metal support. Their colors are uniform, and although they can be applied to precious metals like gold and silver, they are usually applied to copper. They can be applied directly to the metal or on top of a layer of flux. When opaque enamels are layered, the top color will dominate, the opposite of what happens with transparent enamels. Opaque enamels are mainly used for cloisonné work, but they also create very interesting results with painted enamel and champlevé. They can also be very expressive when used in the same piece as transparent enamels, with which they strongly contrast. Opaque enamels come in a much smaller range of colors than transparent ones; the number of available colors varies according to the manufacturer.

Opalescent Enamels

Opalescent enamels are translucent enamels in milky tones between white and blue that show a characteristic sheen, similar to that of wax, with iridescent highlights. Their name refers to the opal, a very popular semiprecious stone that is translucent with a waxy sheen, sometimes with some iridescence. The milky tone of these enamels is also somewhat reminiscent of alabaster. The opalescence results from the diffraction of light caused by particles in the enamel. These very attractive enamels are more difficult to fire than other kinds. Some opalescent enamel colors require two firings in the kiln. During the first, they are fired until the enamel layer

▼ Piece of a transparent enamel disk.

◀ Fragments of clear enamel (flux) (A) and an opalescent enamel (B).

is totally transparent and then allowed to cool. When they are fired again, they are watched carefully until they become opalescent, and then immediately removed from the kiln. It is possible to remove them from the kiln and fire them several times until arriving at the desired effect. Other enamels require just a single phase because they become more opaque with each firing—that is, they become whiter and lose their typical iridescence. If opalescent enamels are applied directly to the metal substrate, they will also lose much of their opalescence, so it is a good idea to apply them over a layer of flux or over transparent colors. A layer may also be applied over previously fired opaque enamels to create a marbleized effect. Opalescent enamels are available in a limited range of colors: whites, pinks, blues, greens, and yellows.

▶ A disk of opaque enamel.

ENAMELS WITH LEAD AND LEAD-FREE ENAMELS

Some enamels are made with lead as a flux and others are made with lead-free fluxes. The former are made for artistic purposes and goldwork. Enamels with lead are sold in containers labeled with the international hazard symbol. The presence of lead carries great health risks for the artist, but the use of proper protective measures will eliminate the danger. You should always be aware of the characteristics of the enamel you are using, and study the technical information supplied by the manufacturer.

It is not possible to say which of these enamels is best for making a work of art, as the final results primarily depend on correctly carrying out the technical processes of enameling. For this reason, enamels with lead and lead-free enamels are equally useful, although there are some considerations you must keep in mind. Generally, **lead-free enamels** can be used with almost any technique, they are cheaper, and they weigh less, so that you get more material than when buying an equal amount of enamel with lead. Also, lead-free opaque enamels usually have a greater tonal range. **Enamels with lead**, however, offer a wider range of colors, which is especially important when working with opalescent enamels. They are also more durable and brighter, which is especially apparent in transparent enamels; their sheen and transparency are greater than those of lead-free enamels, which generally do not look as bright. Enamels from different manufacturers should not be mixed, nor should enamels from different batches, as this can cause problems. Before starting any project, it is important to create a palette (see pages 75–77) to test the usefulness of the enamels, their characteristics, and their behavior.

▼ A disk of opalescent enamel, where we can see the difference between the transparent piece and the opaque piece.

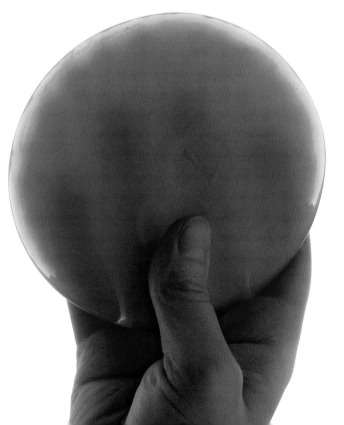

Forms

The Most Common Forms

Granules

After enamel has been manufactured in a kiln, it can either be cooled in the form of disks or cooled in water. The latter method creates small pieces of material in different sizes and with irregular shapes.

Powders

The most common form of enamel, powders are produced by a factory grinding process. Powdered enamel is sold in different particle sizes, 80 mesh (0.149 mm) being the most common. The standard sizes are based on the sizes of the mesh sieves used for sifting and separating the particles. The number of the mesh refers to the number of openings per inch in the standardized metal screen. The size of each sieve is determined by the diameter of the wire used to make the mesh. Number 80 is the most common, but numbers 150 and 200 are also used for transparent enamels, and number 325 is used to separate the finest particles (see the chart below). Some manufacturers make larger grains (40 mesh or less), and it is possible to request special sizes.

Lumps

Lumps are pieces of enamel that are broken into fragments of similar sizes, which vary depending on the method used to break up the enamel disk in the factory. Enamel in lump form is practically inalterable if it is of good quality; kept away from dust and humidity, it is very stable, and it lasts longer than enamel powder and granules. Lumps deteriorate more slowly when exposed to atmospheric agents because the surface is less in proportion to the size of each piece than that of powder and lump enamel, where the surface is greater with respect to the material contained in each particle.

◀ Granules.

▼ Lumps.

PARTICLE MEASURES	
Particle Sizes	Mesh
0.149 mm	80
0.117 mm	100
0.099 mm	150
0.074 mm	200
0.004 mm	325

▼ ▶ Powdered enamels.

Beads

Enamel beads are as small as the head of a pin, or slightly larger. They are used to create surface textures or special decorative effects. They are usually attached to a previously fired layer of enamel with adhesive, melted by firing in a kiln, or mixed with powdered enamel in an applied layer.

Threads

Threads are filaments or fine sticks of enamel. They are sold in a fairly wide range of colors and are quite uniform in length and thickness. They can be used to create interesting decorative effects.

Other Forms

Millefiori

Millefiori is the name for cylinders of mosaic glass. These fairly thick rods are formed by grouping filaments or pieces of different colors that are fired to make shapes. While the glass is still hot, it is cut to make cylindrical pieces with colored decorative shapes appearing in the cross section. Since millefiori are a different type of glass, they require more time in the kiln than enamels, which can be inconvenient. However, they can be used to create some interesting decorative effects and can be combined with the other forms of enamel.

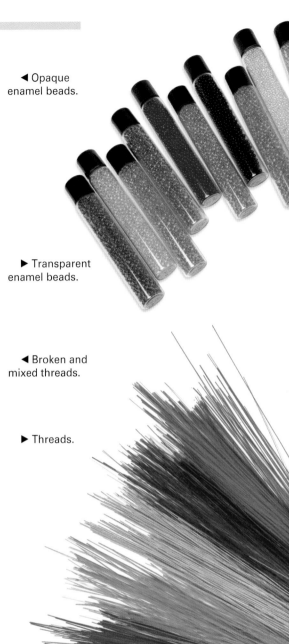

◀ Opaque enamel beads.

▶ Transparent enamel beads.

◀ Broken and mixed threads.

▶ Threads.

▶ Millefiori.

Materials

and Tools

Next, we will take a detailed look at the materials and tools that are used for enameling in the studio. They are grouped according to their use so that you can easily find everything you need to tackle each technical process. We have included a description of each tool and material, an explanation of its possible uses, and, when necessary, advice on safety issues. There is also a separate section on the studio layout and safety, which require special attention when working with enamel. The art of enameling encompasses many processes that demand thorough knowledge of a wide spectrum of materials and tools. Therefore, it is important to know the particular characteristics of your materials and tools, and, when necessary, even the manufacturer's technical information.

Metals

Gold

Gold is a precious metal that is yellow in color and whose chemical symbol is Au. It is the most malleable and ductile of all metals, soft, very heavy, and unaffected by most corrosive agents. Pure gold does not oxidize when it is heated but instead preserves its characteristic color, and its melting point is 1,947.8°F (1,064.33°C). It is an excellent substrate for enameling, but its major drawback is its high cost; thus, it is mainly used for jewelry and by goldsmiths.

Different colors of gold can be created by alloying it with other metals. There are a variety of colors, depending on the alloys used. Red gold is made by mixing gold with a proportion of copper, rose gold with silver and copper, white gold with silver and palladium, and green gold with silver. Eighteen-karat gold, which is mostly used for jewelry, is 75% gold (18 parts gold and 6 of another metal or metals), and 14-karat gold is 58.33% gold (14 parts gold to 10 parts other metal or metals). Some of the metals alloyed with gold, such as copper, oxidize when they are heated, resulting in a dark tone under the enamel that must be removed. The best alloys for enameling are 18-, 20-, 22-, and, of course, pure 24-karat gold.

Silver

Silver is a precious metal whose chemical symbol is Ag. It is white, shiny, ductile, very malleable, and soft. It conducts heat and electricity very well. The purity of silver is measured in thousandths; pure silver contains 999 to 1,000 parts silver. Its melting temperature is 1,763.6°F (962°C), close to the working temperature of enamels, which requires taking precautions during the firing process. It is also very sensitive to changes in temperature, and it can warp and cause the enamel to come off. Like gold, silver alloys oxidize when heated, so alloys with less than 850 parts silver are not adequate for enamelwork. Often, silver alloys with 925 to 960 parts silver are used for enameling. Only fine (pure) silver does not oxidize. In addition, there are other kinds of silver with their own characteristics.

▶ Silver: in sheet (A) and other forms (B).

Sterling Silver

Standard, or sterling, silver is 925 thousandths, or 92.5% pure silver with 7.5% other metal, generally copper, and its melting point is 1,670°F (910°C). Because of its copper content, it oxidizes when it is heated, reducing the transparency and shininess of transparent enamels if they are applied directly on the oxidized silver. To avoid this, sterling silver is deoxidized after annealing, always just before applying the enamel (see page 69). A special kind of silver called bright sterling silver is made with 92.5% pure silver, 6.3% copper, and 1.2% germanium (Ge), with a melting temperature of between 1,409 and 1,607°F (765 and 875°C).

Britania Silver

Britannia silver, or Britannia metal, is purer than silver, an alloy of 96.3% pure silver and 3.6% of another metal, usually copper. Its melting point is between 1,634 and 1,688°F (890 and 920°C). Although it has only half the copper of sterling silver, it oxidizes just the same.

Platinum

Platinum, whose chemical symbol is Pt, is grayish white in color, heavy, malleable, and ductile, and it resists corrosion. It maintains good physical properties at high temperatures, with a melting point of 3,214.4°F (1,768.4°C). Its main inconvenience is its very high price, so its use is somewhat restricted. Its gray color is not the best for use with transparent enamels, and generally there are no enamels made for use with platinum.

▶ Gold.

A

B

Copper

Copper's chemical symbol is Cu, its color is reddish brown, and it is very ductile, malleable, resistant to corrosion, and one of the best conductors of heat. It is less expensive than other metals, it can be recycled any number of times, and it is easily worked. Its melting temperature is 1,981.4°F (1,082°C). Its behavior during firing is predictable, making it an acceptable substrate for enameling. However, copper oxidizes in the presence of heat, forming a black layer of cupric oxide (CuO), which must be removed. Annealed copper is most appropriate for working with enamel. This commercial copper has a minimum purity of 99.9% copper and 200 to 400 ppm (parts per million) oxygen (O). During its manufacture, oxygen is introduced into the copper, producing a very pure commercial copper.

Because of its characteristics and its low cost, copper is the most widely used metal for making artistic enamels. It is sold in various forms and thicknesses, and it is possible to order stamped sheets and spun shapes from the manufacturer.

◀ Sheets of copper: 0.012 in (0.3 mm) (A), 0.024 in (0.6 mm) (B), 0.028 in (0.7 mm) (C), 0.02 in (0.5 mm) (D), and 0.032 in (0.8 mm) (E).

▼ Stamped sheet copper.

▲ Metal clay: paste (A), liquid in a container (B), and in a syringe applicator (C).

▶ High-density metal clay: paste (A), liquid in a container (B), and in a syringe (C).

Steel

The chemical symbol for steel is Fe. Grayish white in color, it is malleable, ductile, very strong, and magnetic, and it oxidizes quickly in the presence of humidity. If it is pure, its melting temperature is 2,800°F (1,538°C); when carbon is added, the melting temperature of the steel alloy is lowered to 2,109°F (1,154°C) (4.3% carbon). Steel that has been treated with an industrial enamel is generally used for enamelwork.

Stainless Steel

Steel is an alloy made of different proportions of iron and carbon. It is a strong material, hard, ductile, and malleable, and it is easily machined, but it oxidizes easily. Depending on the composition of each alloy, its melting temperature varies from 2,500 to 3,000°F (1,375 to 1,650°C). Stainless steel is an alloy of steel with other metals, mainly chrome (Cr) at a minimum of 10.5%, which makes it resistant to oxidation. Some stainless steels also contain nickel (Ni) and molybdenum (Mo). Their melting temperature starts at 2,500°F (1,371°C). It is possible to use them in the studio if they have a previously applied layer of enamel without flux. Special enamels are available for use with stainless steel.

Metal Clay

Metal clay is a relatively new material developed in the 1990s. It is a mixture of microscopic particles of metal suspended in a water-based organic agglutinate or binder, with characteristics similar to those of clay. Silver clay and gold clay are sold in different forms depending on the manufacturer; the silver is more commonly used. Both of them look like clay and can be worked in the same manner as clay. After it dries, metal clay is fired in a kiln at a maximum of 1,652°F (900°C) for a specified amount of time that varies from one manufacturer to another. The binder burns away during the firing, leaving a piece that is approximately 99% pure metal. Firing causes the piece to shrink according to the amount of metal in the mixture, from 28% for the most common clay to 15% and 12% for mixtures with medium and high concentrations of metal. Metal clays are available in three forms: paste, liquid in a container, and ready to use in a syringe applicator. They are sold under the brands PMC and Art Clay.

Forms of Metals

▲ Silver foil (A) and gold foil (B) hammered by hand.

▼ Silver foil (A) and gold foil (B) in books.

B   A

▶ Gold wire.

▼ Copper wire 0.004 in (0.1 mm) thick used by artists in the Republic of Georgia.

Different Types of Metals

Foils

Known as *paillons* in French, foils are very thin sheets of gold or silver, just a few microns thick. The leaves are sold in books, small packets of thin paper with the foils between the pages. They are different from metal leaf in that they are somewhat thicker. They are placed between layers of transparent enamel to create tonal effects, for the color and sheen of the metal itself, and to add luminosity.

Wire

Wire is generally very thin, often with a rectangular cross section, and is often used with the cloisonné technique. It is available on spools or in rolls and in different sizes; the most common is 0.02 inches (0.5 mm) thick and 0.05 inches (1.2 mm) wide, but wire can be made in any size.

Shapes

In addition to sheets, metal pieces, especially copper, are sold in different shapes and sizes, ready for use in the studio after cleaning and preparation. These shapes can be three-dimensional, such as

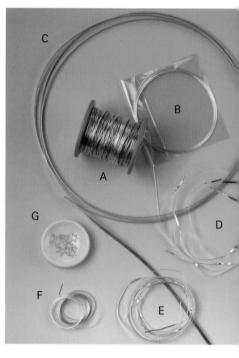

▶ Samples of different silver wire: 0.057 in (0.4 mm) on a spool (A) and in a bag (B), 0.024 in (0.6 mm) thick and 0.02 in (0.5 mm) wide (C), 0.004 in (0.1 mm) Japanese silver (D), 0.008 in (0.2 mm) (E), 0.012 in (0.3 mm) Britannia silver (F), formed pieces (G).

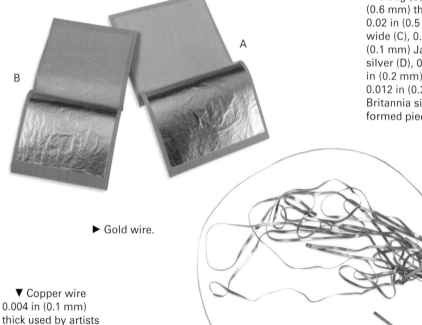

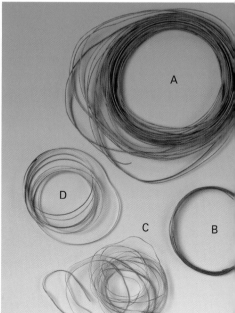

▶ Different samples of copper wire: 0.024 in (0.6 mm) thick (A), 0.031 in (0.8 mm) thick round (B), 0.008 in (0.2 mm) thick and 0.008 in (0.2 mm) wide (C), 0.008 in (0.2 mm) thick and 0.016 in (0.4 mm) wide (D).

bowls, plates, and pedestals, or designed for specific uses, such as beads for making pendants and decorative pieces. It is also possible to special order pieces in particular shapes. Small gold and silver foils, stamped and rolled, are used as decorative elements in certain jewelry work.

Tubes

Gold and silver cylinders are used to create inclusions in enamel. Embedded directly into the layer of enamel, they become part of the enamel piece.

Pre-Enameled Pieces

Iron and steel pieces that have been coated with a layer of industrial enamel are available for use in the enameling studio. Ready to be used, their surfaces are perfectly smooth and even, making them particularly apt for silk screening and decals. Large sheets, which are mainly used for architectural siding, are very stable and resistant to warping.

▲ ▼ Pieces of copper in various forms.

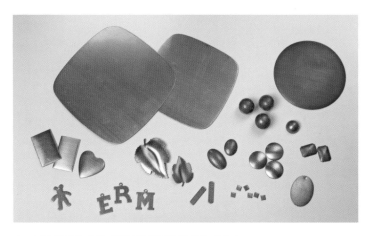

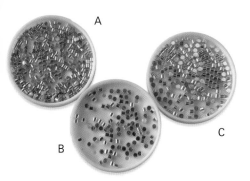

◀ Silver foils with stamped designs.

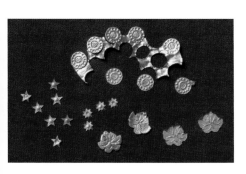

◀ Silver tubes: 0.06 in (1.5 mm) diameter (A), 0.07 in (1.8 mm) diameter (B), and 0.08 in (2 mm) diameter (C).

A

B

C

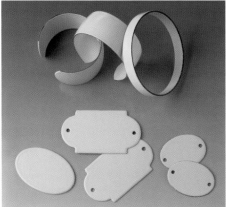

◀ Pre-enameled pieces: bracelets and decorative plaques in steel.

▼ Sheets of pre-enameled steel are available in different sizes and colors.

◀ Formed pieces of industrial enameled steel.

Materials for Cleaning Metals

Chemicals

Nitric Acid

The chemical formula for nitric acid is HNO_3. It is a viscous liquid, between transparent and yellow in color. It is corrosive and toxic, with an acrid odor. It can be diluted with water, but it is a very strong acid and a powerful corrosive agent. It is used for cleaning and deoxidizing metals, especially copper, gold, silver, and their alloys. It is also used for removing surface metal by etching in the champlevé and basse-taille techniques. Pickling compound can be used in its place, but it is only useful for cleaning and not nearly as effective on copper as acid. Nitric acid is also sometimes used to enhance the transparency of some enamels during the cleaning process. It should be used in a well-ventilated place with an air extraction system. A mask with a filter should be used, as well as gloves to avoid contact burns and glasses to protect the eyes from splashing.

Sulfuric Acid

Sulfuric acid's chemical formula is H_2SO_4. Also known as vitriol, it is an oily, viscous, and hygroscopic liquid that is transparent and odorless. A very powerful corrosive agent, it can be diluted with water. It should be used in a well-ventilated area with an air extraction system; tongs or gloves, and safety glasses, are also necessary. It is used for cleaning metals, like silver. Granular dry acid (pickling compound) may be used in its place; it is mainly sodium bisulfate, and can be dissolved in water. Sold under the name

Sparex, pickling compound is safer and works as well as traditional acid. It should not be used with iron and steel.

Bicarbonate

Bicarbonate, also known as bicarbonate of soda and sodium hydrogen carbonate, is a compound with the formula $NaHCO_3$. These white solid crystals are safe for people and the environment and are very water soluble. Bicarbonate reacts with acids to neutralize them, freeing CO_2 as a gas, and it can be used in large quantities because of its harmlessness. It is used in the metal cleaning process to neutralize acids and to remove grease.

Detergent

Liquid dishwashing detergent (a synthetic tensioactive compound) can be used for simple cleaning of metal when it is not necessary or recommended to use acids. It is diluted in water and applied by scrubbing with scouring pads or brushes.

Vinegar

Vinegar is a sour liquid made from wine through acidic fermentation. Its main component is acetic acid (CH_3COOH), which is responsible for its sour flavor and smell. It is water soluble and is mixed with salt to saturation for cleaning metal. It is a good substitute for acid, but it does not work as well.

Salt

Salt is a condiment and food additive that is mainly sodium chloride, whose chemical formula is NaCl. It is used with vinegar for simple cleaning of metal.

Abrasives

Pumice

Finely ground pumice stone is of volcanic origin, composed of approximately 70% silica, 15% alumina or aluminum oxide, and traces of potassium and sodium oxides. It is sold as a whitish powder in different grits, and it is used for cleaning and polishing metals.

◄ Nitric acid.

◄ Liquid dishwashing detergent.

► Vinegar and salt.

Sandpaper

Sandpaper is also called emery paper. It comes as sheets of heavy paper, or sometimes fabric or vulcanized fiber, with an abrasive material bonded to one side. It is sold in different grits and qualities, indicated by a number on the sheet. The higher the number the finer the grit, and the less abrasive the sandpaper. Sandpaper is rubbed on the surface of the metal to eliminate any oxidation or scratches in the final polishing of some enameled pieces.

Abrasive Rubber

Abrasive rubber pads are available in various sizes for cleaning and polishing metal. In certain cases, household steel wool pads may be used for polishing metals.

Brushes

Brushes are also used for cleaning metal. Brushes with synthetic bristles are appropriate for scrubbing metal with bicarbonate in the acid bath method, while brushes with metal bristles are the best for removing resistant oxides (tarnish), especially in hard-to-reach corners. Household scrubbing pads can sometimes be used in place of a brush.

Feathers

Bird feathers are waterproof and do not soak up anything; therefore, they are resistant to acids. They are used to remove small bubbles that form on metal when it is submerged in acid during cleaning. The feather is lightly wiped across the metal to eliminate the bubbles without scratching it. Feathers should be handled with care; avoid touching your skin with the acid solution (gloves must be worn). After use, feathers should be washed with plenty of water.

▲ Sheets of sandpaper.

▼ Brushes with metal bristles (A), brushes with synthetic bristles (B), bicarbonate (C), pumice (D), abrasive rubber pads (E), and natural bird feathers (F).

Special Materials

Serigraphy

Screens

The screens used for serigraphy consist of a frame (a metal or wood stretcher) that holds a mesh with open areas that represent the image that is to be printed. The selected design is applied to the screen as a photo print in a specialized studio. This results in a negative of the impression that the artist wishes to create, with closed areas where the paint will not pass through (the negative space in the original design), and open areas where the paint will pass through to create the impression (the dark areas in the original design). A screen that will assure a high resolution is required for screen-printing on enamel, the best being polyester with 300 threads per inch (120 threads per cm).

Squeegees

Squeegees are made of a thick neoprene, rubber, or polyurethane blade inserted in a wood, plastic, or metal handle of a similar length. They are used to create the impression, pushing the paint through the screen to cover the enamel. The squeegee should be somewhat wider than the image that is being printed.

Screen Printing Oil

To make the screen printed image, a paste is made of vitreous paint and terpineol oil, a transparent, colorless liquid with a characteristically intense odor that is not water soluble. Turpineol is a mixture of products obtained from distilling pine oil. It can irritate the skin and mucous membranes, so it is a good idea to ventilate the room after its use.

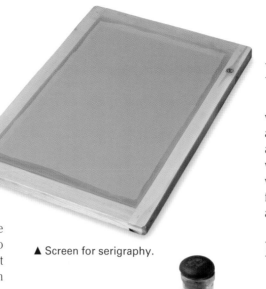

▲ Screen for serigraphy.

▲ Squeegee and terpineol oil.

Decals

A decal is made by mechanically printing vitrifiable inks and paint with an organic agglutinate on paper with a small amount of adhesive, and than covering it with a coat of water-soluble varnish. After being soaked in water, it is placed on an opaque and perfectly smooth enameled substrate. Decals are also used for ceramic and porcelain work.

Industrial Enamels

Industrial enamels are very finely ground, powdered enamels. They are mainly used in industry on iron and steel substrates, but they also can be useful to artists. They are available in powder or liquid paste form; the latter is a water-based solution with a small amount of agglutinate. They can be combined with other non-industrial enamels and applied with an airbrush or a compressed air spray gun in a booth like those used for glazing ceramics.

◀ Selection of decals.

◀ Industrial enamels in barbotine, or slip.

▲ Special adhesive for vertical cloisonné work.

For Cleaning

Ammonia

A colorless liquid with the formula NH_4OH, ammonia has a characteristic strong odor. It is very toxic and gives off fumes that irritate the eyes and mucous membranes. Gloves, eye protection, and a special mask are required for working with ammonia. It is used for removing pastes and grease from polishing, and for cleaning after doing lapidary work.

Acetone

A colorless liquid with the formula CH_3COCH_3, acetone has a characteristic sweetish odor, and it is very volatile. It is a solvent for a large number of commercial adhesives. Its strong odor is easily detectable, making accidental intoxication very rare, but it is quite flammable and must be stored very carefully. Gloves should be worn if it might come into contact with the hands. Like alcohol, it is ideal for removing grease from the surfaces of enamels and metals before applying glue.

For Copying and Making Transfers

Transfer paper, also called carbon paper (black in color), is used to make copies by applying pressure to one side. It is used to transfer designs to the metal support to act as a guide for cutting with the graver or painting with varnish resist for champlevé. White papers are best for transferring to surfaces that are already enameled; their pigment is fixed by a brief firing in the kiln, which removes the oily agglutinate.

For Drying

After they are cleaned, enamels should be placed on an aluminum sheet or tray located below a heat source, like a strong lamp, or on a working kiln, until they are completely dry. This makes them perfectly clean and dry for applying colors by dry sifting. Blotter paper, which is thick, heavy, and spongy, is used to absorb excess moisture from enamels. Kitchen towels can be used for drying surfaces and auxiliary elements. A used cotton rag is also very useful for drying.

For Templates

There are many materials that can be used for making templates: paper and cardboard, rigid plastic, and plastic that will adhere temporarily with static electricity, which is very useful for large areas and spraying vertical pieces in an enameling spray booth. Other common items, like screens and frames, can be used for templates.

◀ Templates made from plastic, cardboard, and reusable electrostatic plastic.

▶ Aluminum sheet (A), transfer papers (B), and blotter papers (C).

Tools for Metal

For Measuring and Marking

Ruler and Square

The ruler and square are used for measuring and drawing designs on metal. The ruler has graduated marks and is mainly used for measuring and drawing straight lines, while the square is used for checking right angles and as an aid for drawing parallel lines.

Compass

The compass with two points, also called dividers, is a steel instrument used for marking curves, circles, and arcs on metal, and also for measuring distances.

Pencil and Scribe

The grease pencil is used for drawing and marking on metal, and it burns away in the annealing process prior to enameling. There are also special pencils for marking enameled surfaces; their lines disappear when enamels applied dry over them are fired. The scribe is also used for marking metal, and for removing oxides by scraping.

For Filing and Cutting

Metal Shears

Shears are used for cutting sheets of metal. Hand shears are used for thinner sheet metal, and there are different sizes to choose from based on the metal thickness. Small hand shears are used for the thinnest sheets, and they are also good for cutting out complicated shapes and small details. Larger shears are used for thicker sheets, and special curved shears are used for cutting curved shapes. When cutting, the shears are moved forward without closing them all the way to the points, which would create a mark in the metal that might hinder later processes.

The guillotine-style table shear has a large blade that makes long, straight cuts. It can cut a large number of pieces efficiently, and perfectly square if required. It should not be used on sheets that surpass the maximum thickness indicated by the manufacturer or problems may occur. Saws should be used on sheet metal thicker than $\frac{3}{64}$ inch (1 mm).

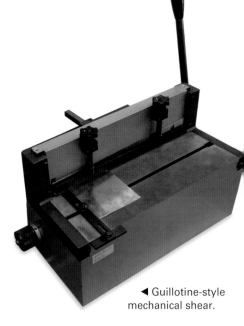

◀ Guillotine-style mechanical shear.

Files and Jeweler's Files

Files are used for touching up and finishing metal, for removing burrs, and for repairing defects. Small jeweler's files with different sections (triangular, rectangular, oval, and so on), are very useful and allow you to access difficult corners. Rat-tail files have a cylindrical section that narrows to a point.

▼ Compass (A), square (B), ruler (C), grease pencil for marking metal (D), scribe (E), shears for thin sheets and details (F), medium shears (G), heavy shears for thick sheets (H).

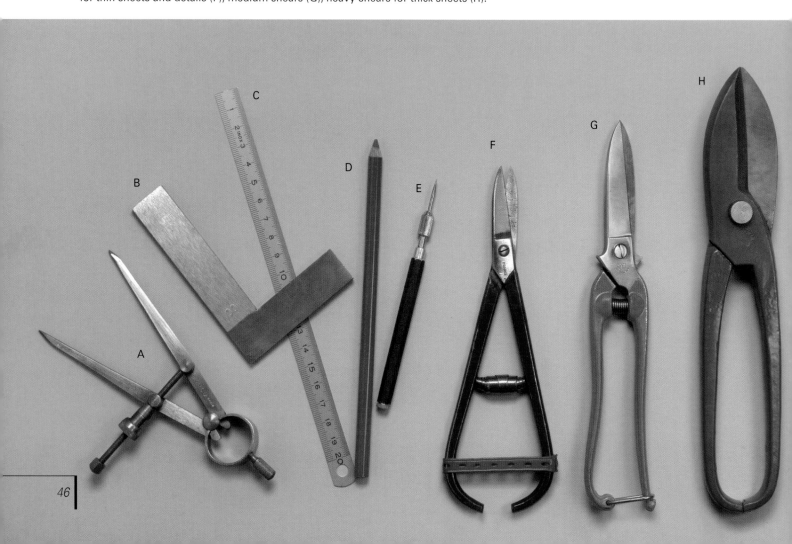

Hand Drill

A hand drill is used to make holes in metal. The sheet metal must be fixed to the worktable before using the drill. It is important to mark the point where you wish to drill with a scribe or awl to keep the bit from slipping across the sheet and making marks and scratches. The best bits for studio work range from 3/64 to 3/16 in (1 to 5 mm), although in jewelry work bits smaller than 3/64 in (1 mm) can be used.

Jeweler's Saw

A jeweler's saw consists of a very fine blade vertically mounted in a metal frame. The blades, which have different thicknesses and numbers of teeth, are held perfectly straight in the frame by clamps at each end. This tool is used for cutting metal sheets that are thicker than 1/64 inch and in cases where a very complicated shape must be cut out and it is not possible to do it from the outside with shears. Cutting is done by holding the blade exactly vertical to the metal while pushing with a down and forward motion.

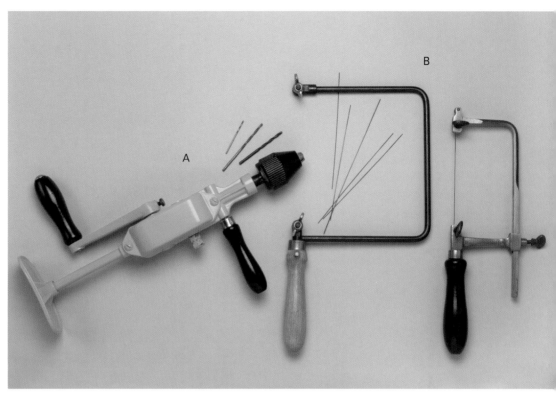

▲ Hand drill and bits (A), jeweler's saw and blades (B).

▼ Handle and blades (A) and a selection of files (B).

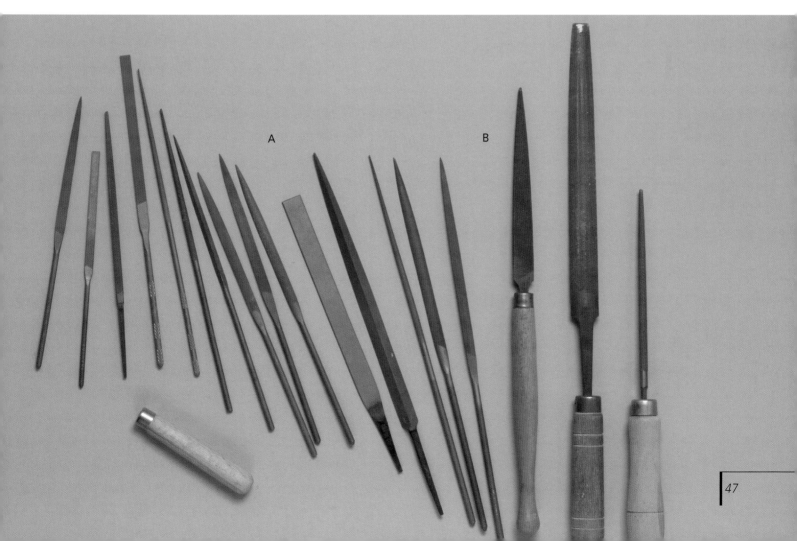

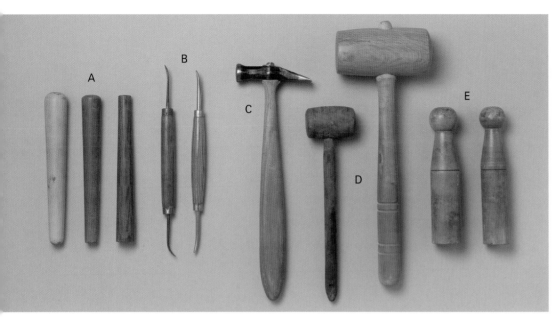

▲ Dapping tools in wood (A), metal burnishing tools (B), planishing hammer (C), mallets (D), and wood dapping tools (E).

metal head with rounded faces, one of them with a slight curve. The center part of the face is used to strike the metal to give it a hammered texture.

Wood Mallets

Wood mallets are used for forming, correcting, and flattening metal without leaving marks, and for shaping sheet metal on large wood block molds. They are made of hardwoods and sometimes have a nylon head.

Bench Block

A bench block is a steel plate, usually square, with straight polished sides, that is used like an anvil to support sheet metal as it is worked and shaped.

Molds

Molds are used for shaping metal sheets. They can be wood—which you can make, have custom made, or buy off the shelf—or steel blocks that have shapes of different sizes, like hemispheres and channels.

Burnishing Tools

Burnishing tools are used to finish metal—especially gold and silver—by rubbing it, making it look shiny and polished. They consist of wood handles with an agate tip at one end, which can be curved or flat but is always very polished. They can also be made of steel.

Pliers

Pliers are small tools with square or conical jaws that are used to cut, bend, and form metal wire for the cloisonné technique. The

For Forming

Dapping Punches

Dapping punches are used to make convex shapes of varying sizes by hand on a steel block. They are used with thin sheet metal up to $\frac{1}{64}$ inch (0.4 mm). By applying pressure to the metal on a soft support, the artist can make sure that the piece will only come into contact with the firing support at the edges, keeping it from bonding to the enamel. This also makes the sheet rigid and less likely to warp during firing. It can help avoid unfortunate shiny spots in the center of the composition when the piece is finished. Dapping

tools can be metal or wood. Wood dapping tools with slightly rounded ends are used for giving a general shape to metal pieces. Tools with spherical ends are used with the metal dapping block and tapped with a mallet. Burnishing tools consist of a central handle with a curved metal piece at each end. They are used to reach corners and angles and for outlining the piece, making sure that the edges sit perfectly flat on the plane.

Planishing Hammer

The planishing hammer is used for forming metals thicker than $\frac{1}{64}$ in (0.4 mm), striking the sheet metal on a metal block. It has a

▼ A set of pliers (A), cutters (B), tweezers (C), and planishing hammer (D).

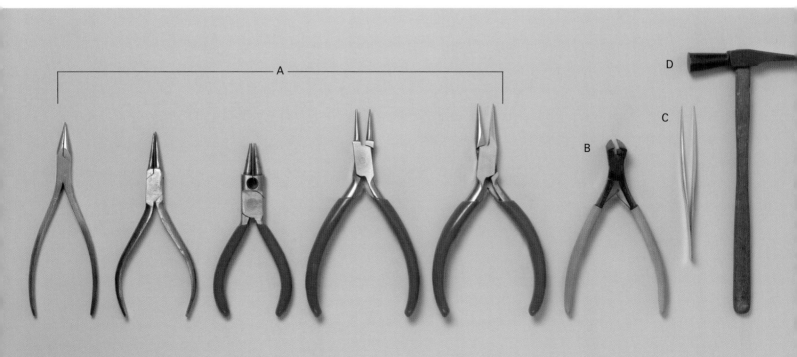

◄ Steel dapping block, with several hemispherical molds of different sizes, and a wood block.

▶ Bench block.

▲ Agate burnishing tools.

wire is shaped using pliers with smooth jaws, while pliers with straight, sharp edges are used for cutting the wire.

Tweezers

Tweezers are very useful for shaping, picking up, and holding pieces of shaped wire on the metal support in the cloisonné technique, and for holding and manipulating foils. Jeweler's tweezers, which open when squeezed, are very useful for holding small pieces of jewelry during the enameling process.

Goldsmith's Hammer

The small goldsmith's hammer is used to flatten metal wire used for cloisonné and for shaping very small pieces.

Chasing Tools

Used for chiseling and chasing, chasing tools are steel punches with prismatic sections that create bas-relief forms in the metal. Held perpendicular to the surface of the metal, the end of the tool is struck with a hammer to model the shapes.

Chasing Hammer

A chasing hammer is used for striking metal chisels and punches. It has an ergonomic wood handle that makes it comfortable to hold.

Gravers

Gravers are tools with steel blades that have a cutting point at one end. They are used to cut, engrave, and remove metal in the champlevé and bas-relief techniques. Practice is required to master using them. The cutting is done with the tip of the blade, pushing forward and keeping the hand that is holding the metal plate behind the one with the tool. Metal is removed by making small cuts, rais-

ing metal slivers, and working the area little by little. The point of the blade should always be kept very sharp.

Whetstone

There are many stones for sharpening gravers, and the best ones are known as Arkansas stones. These are sedimentary stone composed mainly of microcrystalline silica. They are dense, very hard, white to gray-white, and translucent, and they have a typical cerulean shine. Nevertheless, they are very fragile and are easily broken. Sometimes they are called novaculite. A lubricating oil must be used when using them.

▼ Punch (A), chasing hammer (B), set of gravers (C), and whetstone (D).

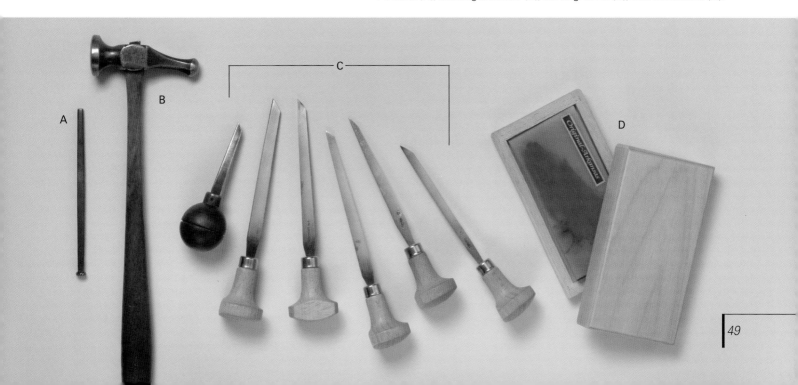

Tools for Applying Enamel

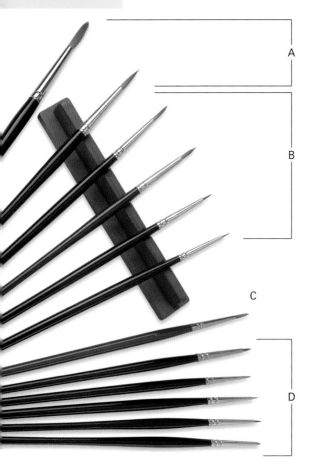

▲ Sable brushes for enamel counter coats and large pieces (A), sable brushes for painting (B), synthetic brush for painting (C), and conical sable brushes for painting on enamel and miniature work (D).

Different Application Tools

Brushes

Brushes are used for applying wet enamels. It is a good idea to have a large selection of brushes, each one for a specific use. The best ones for enameling are made of sable hair, which is very soft, flexible, absorbent, and durable. Among these, brushes with fine, conical tips are the best for painting miniature enamels, medium sizes for applying counter coats, and large sizes for large pieces and counter coats. They should be washed with distilled water and left to dry completely after each use. Store them carefully to avoid damaging the tips.

Needles and Steel Points

Steel points with wood handles are very useful for spreading and adjusting the positioning of enamel granules during wet applications. It is good to have several sizes. These tools can be made by inserting needles into a wood handle according to your needs.

Spatulas

Spatulas are necessary for applying wet enamel. They are made of steel with tips on each end of a handle. The tips can be flat, round, or in spoon, lance, or other shapes. Spatulas for transporting enamel (see page 55) are made of a flat, rigid steel blade and a handle that is usually wood. Those used for mixing enamel paste have flat, flexible blades that can be long, triangular, or pointed. They are also useful for transporting and manipulating small pieces to avoid touching them with your hands.

Nib Pens

Nib pens are used for small touch-ups or for applying wet enamel like brushes and spatulas.

Sticks and Trays

Trays are used for holding pieces while applying wet enamel and for transporting them to the kiln later. They are usually made of wood or Masonite and have a resin coating (like melamine) to make them water resistant. They allow the pieces to be moved and turned as needed without touching them. It helps to place the work on small wood sticks so that it does not come into contact with the tray; this also makes it easier to pick up the piece with a spatula for transporting.

Bridge

A piece of wood shaped like a bridge is used for resting your hand, and for keeping you from wiping your hand across large pieces and damaging them. It can be made in the studio or custom made according to your needs; the size of the bridge should always be appropriate for the dimensions of each enamel piece.

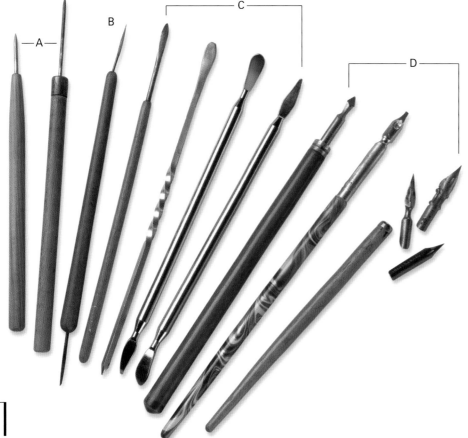

◄ Steel points for applying and spreading enamel (A), tool with needles made in the studio (B), spatulas (C), and nib pens (D).

▼ Spatulas for mixing and transporting enamel.

Protectors

When working with wet enamels, it is important to have a range of protective glass covers, like those used in laboratories. They protect the enamel during breaks in the working process, keeping dust and dirt off the pieces. They are especially useful for working with miniatures that require a long time to create.

Containers and Bottles

It is a good idea to have some porcelain or glass containers for working with wet enamels, as they are useful for holding the distilled water used for wetting and cleaning the brushes. Containers are also needed for dispensing small amounts of distilled water (for example, a small squirt bottle). Small glass or plastic containers with wide mouths and screw caps are required for wet enamels.

Screens

Sieves have very fine mesh screens in particular sizes. They are used with dry enamels to deposit the particles on the piece by sifting. They are also used for cleaning the dry enamels, separating them by grain size.

Atomizer

An atomizer is a small bottle, usually plastic, with a spray mechanism for squirting water to lightly and evenly wet the surface of the enamel. It is used to moisten enamel applied dry with distilled water.

◀ Bridge (A), sticks and trays for working and transporting (B), and glass anti-dust protective covers (C).

◀ Spouted bottle for dispensing distilled water.

▼ A collection of containers for distilled water (A), containers and bottles for wet enamel (B), and a plastic container with a spout for filling small containers (C).

▶ A group of screens.

▶ Atomizer.

51

Special Tools and Machines

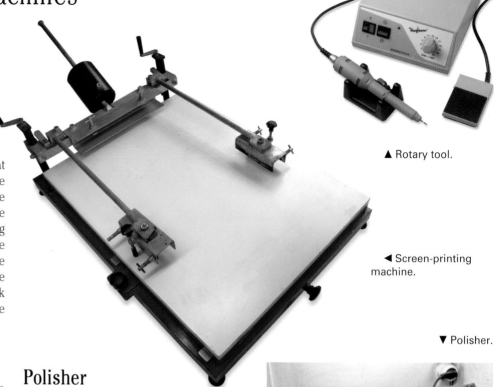

Screen-Printing Machine

A screen-printing machine is used for printing with the serigraphy technique. It consists of a horizontal metal frame fitted with a board with a synthetic surface that is water and oil resistant, and a counterweight with two arms that support the screen. The underside of the frame has adjustable feet that allow the base to sit perfectly level. The counterweight at the back of the base can be adjusted according to the weight of the screen. It is also possible to adjust the locations of the supports where they attach to each side of the screen. The screen is held firmly by the arms and the back part of the device. Its height can then be adjusted using the side screws on the arms.

▲ Rotary tool.

◀ Screen-printing machine.

Rotary Tool

A rotary tool is a small power tool that can hold innumerable drill bits, discs, and grinding bits in a collet for drilling, grinding, sanding, and polishing, among other things. Thanks to a powerful motor, these tools rotate at a very high speed, allowing for fast, precise work. The motorized tool has a long cord to make working more comfortable, and it is controlled by a pedal on the floor. The body is lightweight and ergonomically designed, and the bits can be changed quickly with just a quarter turn of the head holding them in place. Some models have a variable speed control, the ability to rotate in either direction, and a micro-hammer function with controls for force and striking frequency.

Polisher

A polisher, which must be attached to a bench or work surface, has a powerful motor to turn brushes, sandpaper, or wheels that rotate at great speed. It is used for the final polishing and smoothing of some enamelwork and for finishing the metal parts of enameled jewelry that can be seen. A protective shield should be used to keep the walls clean, and a soft covering is advisable for the walls of the booth or space where the polisher is used.

Sandblasting Machine

A sandblasting machine is used for finishing enamelwork. It sprays very fine abrasive material with compressed air to clean the sur-

▼ Polisher.

face of the enamel or metal. It consists of an enclosed box with a compressed air gun to spray the abrasives and a vacuum system for collecting the particles. The box has a window on top so the whole interior can be seen, and there are openings on each side for the user's hands. Some machines are also illumi-

▼ Collets (A), diamond tip grinding bits and diamond tip drill bits (B), steel cutting bits (C), and steel drill bits (D).

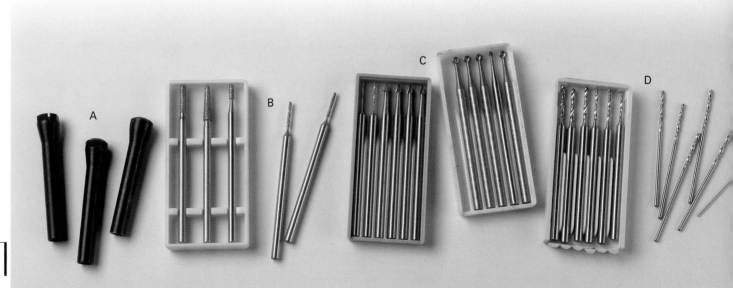

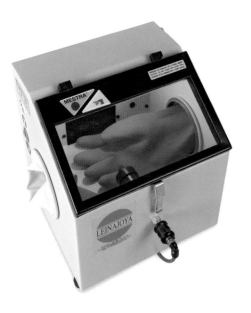

◀ Tabletop sandblasting machine for working with enamel pieces.

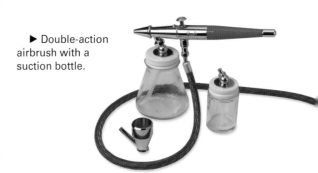

▶ Lapidary machine, here with a polishing wheel.

Lapidary Machine

An electric lapidary machine is very useful for grinding and polishing very thick pieces or pieces with large surfaces, and for mass production. It has a powerful vertical motor with an abrasive disk that rotates at a high speed. It can be used for polishing by changing the disk. The better lapidary machines also have a water-dispensing feature.

Airbrush

An airbrush works like a compressed air gun for applying paint. Its head is shaped like a pen with a tiny needle inside; a compressed air injector that mixes air with the paint is located in a connected receptacle. A tube at the back of the head connects to the compressor, which is regulated with a switch or a lever. Airbrushes are available in single-action and double-action models, but the latter are preferable because they allow the artist to regulate the flow of paint and to control the width of the spray pattern at the same time. There are also two types of paint containers, gravity feed and suction. The first is located at the top of the brush and allows vertical and horizontal work. Although it loses barely any paint, its main drawback is that it is fixed in place and must be cleaned at the same time as the brush. Containers that work by suction are

▶ Double-action airbrush with a suction bottle.

nated. Before starting work, the door is closed tightly and not opened until the task is finished, after waiting at least one minute to be sure that all the abrasives have been removed by the vacuum motor. Some practice is required to use the sandblasting machine. It is a good idea to practice as many times as needed on enamel samples before beginning work on any object. There are also several general rules that you should follow. Pieces should never be held closer to the gun than is recommended by the manufacturer. The abrasives must hit the enamel piece at a specific angle, making it important to work very carefully with objects that have curved surfaces. It is best to regularly check the progress of the work, removing the piece from the spray box to examine it. It is also important to check the state and adhesion of the reserves or masks, if there are any.

attached below the airbrush. They are removable and can be changed, making it easier to clean them and the brush itself. Its main drawback is that it loses some paint each time it is used, and some models make it difficult to paint horizontally. Airbrushing requires some practice to achieve the desired results. It is a precision instrument and very delicate, so it must be carefully cleaned after each use according to the manufacturer's instructions. Incorrect or insufficient cleaning can affect its performance and your work. In enameling, it is used for applying industrial enamels, liquid enamels, and superfine enamels. Large airbrushes are ideal for covering large surfaces, and small ones for precision work.

▼ Carbon steel bits (A), carborundum bits (B), tungsten bits (C), mandrel and sandpaper (D), and elastic rubber tips for polishing (E).

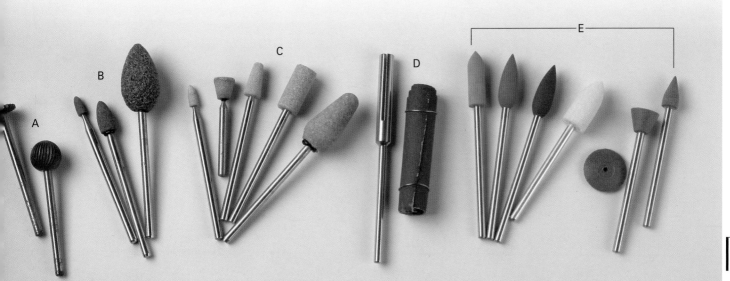

Kilns and Equipment for Firing

Kilns

The kiln is probably the most important element in the studio. Kilns consist of a metal frame that holds an insulated metal box. This box contains an oven made of ceramic fibers that are extremely insulating and thermally stable. Inside the oven, several resistors are located in the top, sides, and bottom; in some models, these are covered with mineral or ceramic fiber plaques. An electric current passes through the resistors to generate radiated heat, which fills the interior of the kiln and the ceramic lining through conduction and radiation. It can reach temperatures of nearly 2,012°F (1,100°C). Tabletop models, with downward-opening counter weighted doors, work as well for small pieces as kilns designed for larger work. Depending on the model and manufacturer, kilns may have a thermometer, a probe inside that connects to a temperature gauge, or a temperature regulator or thermostat that maintains a constant temperature by turning the electric current off and on.

Other Equipment

Ceramic Fiber Planche

A planche made of ceramic fibers bonded with alumina and silica is used as a base for firing enamelwork in the kiln. It is easy to cut with a craft knife or cutter. The organic agglutinate in the ceramic fibers can alter the enamel, causing a matte or muddy finish, so the planche must be fired before it is used. The ceramic fibers will blacken during this firing from the combustion of the organic binder and will expel odorous fumes. They are not noxious, but it is a good idea to ventilate the studio and to use a dust mask and protective gloves. After the adhesive has been burned away, the ceramic fiber planche becomes white again and is ready for use. Before firing, a coating of kaolin mixed with water should be applied and allowed to dry to protect the planche and make it stronger.

Refractory Clay

Refractory clay is very resistant to heat, with a high melting point between 2,912 and 3,182°F (1,600 and 1,750°C). This kind of clay

▲ Ceramic fiber planche.

is very pure and has practically no iron, but it does contain kaolin (the basic material of clays, Al_2O_3. SiO_2. $2H_2O$), and alumina in elevated amounts. It is used as an insulator, in the form of a paste made with water, to protect soldered joints and small jewelry pieces from the heat. Support molds for special enamel pieces can also be made with it.

▶ Tabletop kiln with a door that opens vertically.

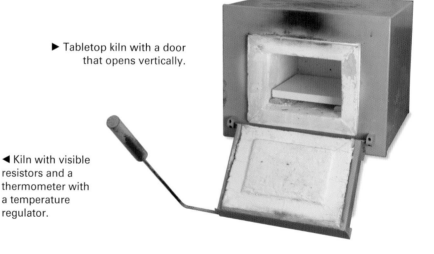

◀ Kiln with visible resistors and a thermometer with a temperature regulator.

▼ Kiln with rollers for inserting and removing large pieces.

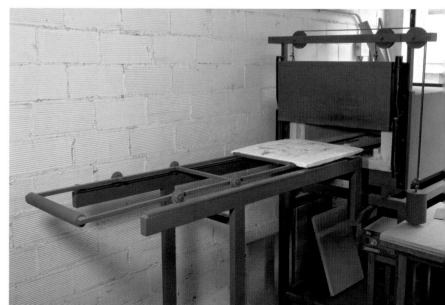

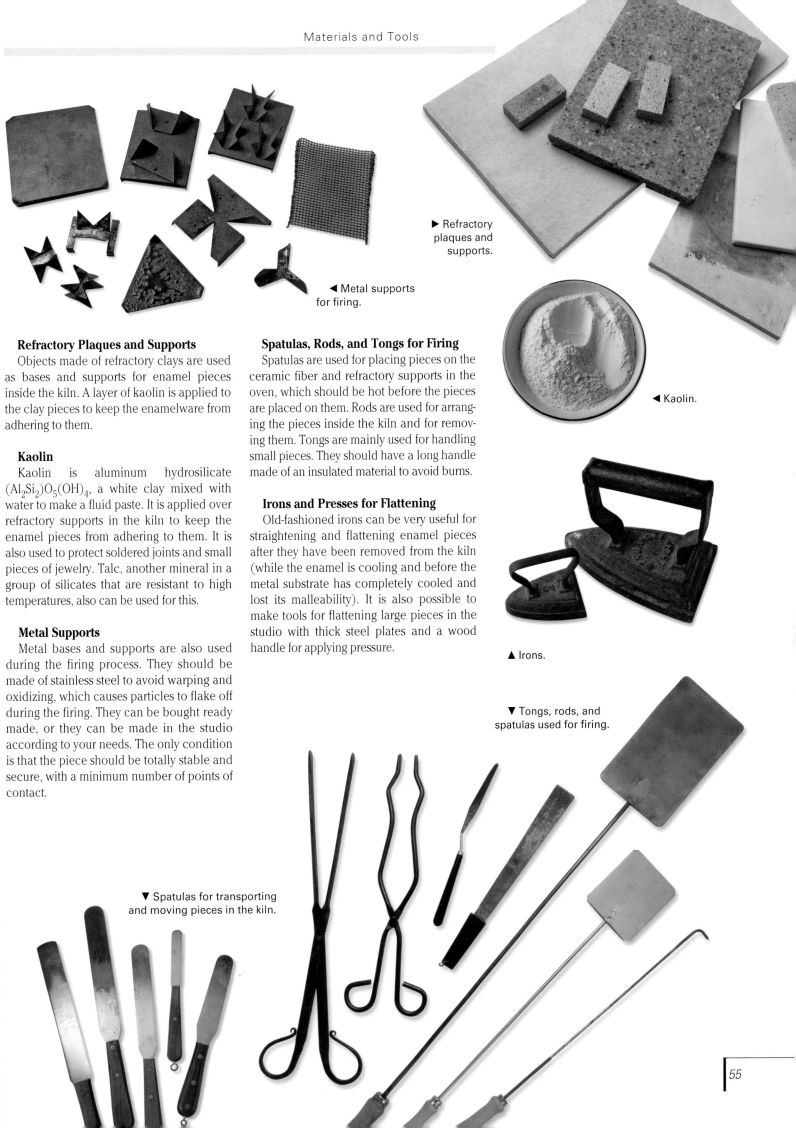

▶ Refractory plaques and supports.

◀ Metal supports for firing.

◀ Kaolin.

Refractory Plaques and Supports

Objects made of refractory clays are used as bases and supports for enamel pieces inside the kiln. A layer of kaolin is applied to the clay pieces to keep the enamelware from adhering to them.

Kaolin

Kaolin is aluminum hydrosilicate $(Al_2Si_2)O_5(OH)_4$, a white clay mixed with water to make a fluid paste. It is applied over refractory supports in the kiln to keep the enamel pieces from adhering to them. It is also used to protect soldered joints and small pieces of jewelry. Talc, another mineral in a group of silicates that are resistant to high temperatures, also can be used for this.

Metal Supports

Metal bases and supports are also used during the firing process. They should be made of stainless steel to avoid warping and oxidizing, which causes particles to flake off during the firing. They can be bought ready made, or they can be made in the studio according to your needs. The only condition is that the piece should be totally stable and secure, with a minimum number of points of contact.

Spatulas, Rods, and Tongs for Firing

Spatulas are used for placing pieces on the ceramic fiber and refractory supports in the oven, which should be hot before the pieces are placed on them. Rods are used for arranging the pieces inside the kiln and for removing them. Tongs are mainly used for handling small pieces. They should have a long handle made of an insulated material to avoid burns.

Irons and Presses for Flattening

Old-fashioned irons can be very useful for straightening and flattening enamel pieces after they have been removed from the kiln (while the enamel is cooling and before the metal substrate has completely cooled and lost its malleability). It is also possible to make tools for flattening large pieces in the studio with thick steel plates and a wood handle for applying pressure.

▲ Irons.

▼ Tongs, rods, and spatulas used for firing.

▼ Spatulas for transporting and moving pieces in the kiln.

The Studio

The Studio Space and Its Layout

The enameling studio should be properly laid out, well organized, and clean. The ideal is to have a large, well-ventilated, and well-lit space. Its size and layout will depend on the work techniques used and the number of people involved in them. The space should be large enough for you to work and store products and materials, as well as finished pieces, comfortably. It should have several separate areas for different enameling processes.

Preferably, the worktable should be located in an area with natural light that is clean and free of dust and drafts. It should be sufficiently large for you to work comfortably, perfectly level, and made of an easy-to-clean material. It should have task lighting and drawers for storing tools. Jars of enamels should have a separate storage shelf that is easy to reach, and they should be labeled by type, color, brand, or manufacturer. Another area should be designated for storing powdered enamels in plastic or glass jars.

Preferably, the kiln should be placed in a separate space. It should have the appropriate electrical wiring with a ground fault interrupter, and be large enough for your enamelwork. The overhead light should have a dimmer to adjust the lighting for different needs, such as darkening the room to watch the color changes that indicate the temperature of the kiln. There should be a side table and a handheld vacuum cleaner in the studio as well.

You will also need a separate space to work with metal. This should include a worktable or bench, as well as furniture to store all the tools and equipment.

Finally, a separate space should be reserved for cleaning enamels and working with sifters and acids. This space should have a sink with running water and a drain, and preferably several work surfaces, one of them with a powerful ventilation system.

It is essential to keep the studio clean and free of dust at all times. Cleaning should be done with a vacuum cleaner that does not release particles of dust and enamel into the air.

▼ The studio should be properly laid out. To clean the enamels, a sink with running water will be needed, as well as a jug of distilled water with a dispenser and an area to store all the tools. Dry enamels should be stored in order and properly labeled (studio of Andreu Vilasís, Barcelona, Spain).

Lighting

The lighting in the studio should be evenly distributed. In addition to the overhead lighting, the studio should have task lights for specific needs. Also, there should be several electrical outlets throughout the work areas.

Safety

Hazardous materials, such as acids, should be stored separately—if possible, inside a special locked cabinet—away from heat sources. The containers should be closed tightly to avoid possible evaporation and stored so that the toxicity logo is visible when opening the cabinet. The studio should have sufficient fire extinguishers and a first aid kit, both of which should be placed in a location that is visible and easy to access. Emergency numbers should also be visible and placed near the telephone. It is important to have a file cabinet to store the technical and safety specifications of all hazardous materials you use; the products should be discarded according to local regulations. The studio must also have the necessary personal protection gear, enough for everyone working in the shop. The proper mask, with regulation, non-expired filters, should be used for each procedure. Tongs or nitrile gloves should be used to handle acids, and special fireproof gloves for the kiln. Depending on the frequency or length of exposure to the kiln, glasses equipped with a total (blue) filter should be used to look inside.

▲ Interior of an enameling classroom (the Llotja School, Barcelona, Spain). The table is large and easy to clean, and it is equipped with a system that allows the projects to be propped up and properly lit.

▲ It is a good idea to have a shelf or drawers with dividers to arrange jars of wet enamel near the worktable. They should be properly labeled, tightly closed, and well organized at all times.

◀ Face mask with filter (A), fireproof gloves for the kiln (B), and nitrile gloves (C).

▶ The studio should have a well-supplied first aid kit that includes a lotion for burns and all the most up-to-date pharmaceutical supplies. It should be placed in a location that is visible and easy to access.

Working with fired enamel requires knowledge of certain key concepts. Unless you understand these concepts, any attempt at creating work will be very difficult, if not impossible. So before attempting enamel techniques, it is important to understand the theory and the practical processes on which enameling is based. Once you understand the basics, it will be easier to put the different techniques into practice, and your knowledge will serve as a valuable reference when experimenting with new methods and creating work in your own style. In the first part of the chapter, we explain the basic theories of enameling and the general practical approaches that underlie the different techniques. In the second, we show the basic techniques of enameling from a practical point of view, including clear, detailed explanations of all the processes involved. Each technique has different characteristics and employs specific processes that influence the working method. In addition, we address certain problems that can come up during the enameling process and offer solutions for each case.

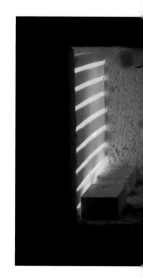

Technical Processes

*B*efore starting to work, it is very important to understand the basic concepts that define the characteristics and behavior of enamels, and to be aware of the crucial processes required to successfully carry out the work, like preparing and cleaning the enamels and metals, applying the enamel, and creating palettes and color samples.

Characteristics and Behavior of Enamel

The behavior of enamels is governed by their peculiar physical characteristics, which in turn are governed by their molecular structures; their amorphous solid structure is the reason for their special qualities and their behavior during firing in the kiln. The nature of the metal support also affects the characteristics of the work.

The Coefficient of Expansion

The coefficient of expansion is the number that expresses the percentage of the expansion of the enamel in relation to the temperature. Enamel changes in size for each degree the temperature goes up. So the larger the coefficient of expansion, the greater the expansion of the enamel. This parameter describes the compatibility of the enamel and the metal substrate.

Viscosity

Viscosity is a characteristic of fluids, especially liquids. It is the resistance of the fluid to the relative movements of its molecules, its resistance to flowing. Viscosity directly depends on and varies with the temperature. In enamels, an increase in temperature decreases their viscosity—that is, their molecules increase their movements and cause the enamel to become more fluid. At higher temperatures there is less viscosity and more fluidity. When they cool to room temperature, the molecules slow down so much that they never find the proper order to form a crystalline solid, so they maintain the amorphous structure of an overcooled liquid, and the enamel is still homogenous when it hardens.

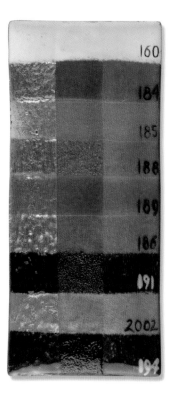

▲ Hardness palette for transparent enamels. The vertical strip in the middle indicates the hardness of the enamels. The rough areas (numbers 191, 188, and 194) show a greater hardness than the enamel selected as a sample, the medium white number 160.

◄ In this palette, the white color of the lower part looks like it is on the surface, since the mauve is much more viscous and is distributed irregularly over it.

Fusibility

Fusibility refers to the point at which a solid will melt—that is, suddenly change from a solid to a liquid state at a given temperature. This is called the **fusion point**, and every material has its own specific fusion point. However, when enamel is heated it softens and becomes fluid without experiencing any abrupt change. Its molecules move freely and allow it to flow. Upon cooling, the molecules slow down little by little and become fixed in a disorderly fashion.

MELTING TEMPERATURES OF ENAMELS	
Kind of Enamel	**Approximate Temperature Range**
Hard	From 1,560 to 1,740°F (850 to 950°C)
Medium (the most common)	From 1,380 to 1,560°F (750 to 850°C)
Soft	From 1,200 to 1,290°F (650 to 700°C)
These temperature ranges are approximate and vary according to the enamel and manufacturer.	
These are general indications, as the firing process relies on a correct combination of time and temperature (see section on firing).	

Hardness

Enamels can be hard, soft, or have a medium hardness depending on their melting temperature. This is usually referred to as the fusion point, which is indeterminate in enamels. Just like all other types of glass, and unlike all other solids, enamel gradually becomes fluid as the temperature rises; the passage from a solid to a liquid state is very slow and even as the fluidity increases.

The hardness of enamels influences the firing process, since at a determined temperature a soft enamel will require less firing time than a hard one (see the section on firing).

The behavior of enamels, then, depends on their hardness but also on their viscosity. It is possible that two different enamels have the same hardness but that one becomes less viscous (and therefore more fluid) than the other at the same temperature. It is best to put a layer of soft enamel with low viscosity over a layer of hard enamel with more viscosity. If hard enamel is put over a layer of softer enamel, the latter will tend to flow and pass through the hard enamel to appear on the surface. This phenomenon can be used to create interesting effects in enamelwork.

Isotropy

When enamel cools, the mobility of the molecules is reduced, and once the material hardens they become fixed in random patterns, resulting in a solid with a molecular structure that is more similar to liquids than to solids. This amorphous structure determines one of enamel's most peculiar physical qualities: isotropy. In isotropic materials like enamels, the physical properties are constant

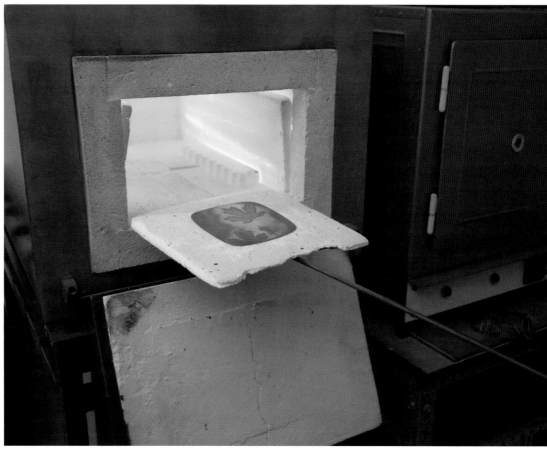

▲ After firing, the enamel slowly cools to room temperature, and as it hardens it acquires the amorphous structure of a supercooled liquid while conserving its homogeneity.

in all directions; that is to say, they act the same no matter what direction we consider. This property allows enamel to form walls, like stained glass.

Firing

Firing is the combination of two parameters: **time** and **temperature**. Both are of equal importance, and if one of them fails, it will cause major problems and may even destroy the work. The enamel is placed in a kiln, that has been preheated to a regulated working temperature, usually about 1,650°F (900°C). Proper firing depends on the amount of time the piece spends in the kiln. There are no fixed rules regarding the necessary time, but it runs from 1 to 5 minutes. The firing of enamels is fast compared to that of glass and ceramics. The amount of time depends on the techniques used, the materials, the size of the piece, the type of metal and its thickness, the hardness of the enamels, their size in relation to the kiln, and so forth.

Softening Point and Melting Point

Enamel quickly reaches its **softening point** in the kiln. This point is the temperature at which the viscosity of the enamel diminishes, and the enamel turns fluid and adheres to the surface of the metal. Then its viscosity gradually decreases and it becomes very fluid, until it reaches the **melting point** (not to be confused with the fusion point), when the enamel particles are completely melted and the surface of the layer becomes perfectly smooth. When the firing is complete, the enamel is removed from the kiln; it will be soft and fluid until it cools. At this point, we see its definitive aspect, a smooth and shiny layer.

▲ This bowl was made by Montserrat Aguasca using the stained glass technique. The isotropic properties of enamel allowed the creation of the walls.

Grain Sizes

The grain or particle sizes of the enamel also influence the firing process. It is important to control the size of the particles because of the way they behave in the kiln. The smaller the grains, the less firing time is required, and the larger they are, the more firing time they require. However, the firing time and final results also depend on other factors besides grain size—for example, the size of the piece and the chemical composition of each enamel used. The particles also determine the transparency of the enamel. This is easy to understand if we keep in mind that the grains of enamel are irregular and have numerous facets. The smaller the pieces, the greater the amount needed to cover a given area, and therefore the number of unions or bonds between the grains will be greater. Conversely, fewer large particles would be needed to cover the same area, and there would be fewer unions. The spaces between the particles can cause bubbles to appear in the enamel when it is fired. The bubbles will be smaller and more numerous if the particles are small, and fewer but larger in size if large particles are used. However, the number of bubbles also depends on the amount of enamel applied; there will be more of them with a larger quantity of enamel. The bubbles cannot be seen with the naked eye if the enamel is of good quality. If there are impurities, they will find spaces between the particles to escape, or they will burn out and create bubbles and spaces, which are difficult to fix. Clearly, cleaning enamels is very important to avoid this problem.

Behavior of Enamel

During firing, enamels pass through three successive phases. First, the granules adhere to the support, maintaining their original shapes, which shows up as a granulated texture with a darkened color. Then the particles join and the texture becomes wrinkled and the color warmer. Finally, the enamel is **completely melted**, at which point the metal acquires its definitive look, a smooth, shiny surface with an orange color. Recognizing these three phases is basic to being able to fire successfully. During the process, it is a good idea to observe the piece inside the kiln, to control the changes in color and texture. Controlling these phases also helps create textural effects in the pieces.

Behavior of the Metal Support

During firing, the enamel gradually becomes fluid while the metal support stays solid. Metals have a fusion point, a specific temperature at which they quickly pass from a solid state to a liquid state. Logically, the fusion points of most of the metals used for enamelwork are higher than the temperature that the kiln reaches, so there is no problem. However, silver has a melting point that is very near that of enamels, so precautions must be taken during firing (see pages 122–123).

During firing, metal expands as a result of the high temperature. In solids, molecules are fixed and only vibrate around their point of equilibrium. The increase in thermal energy (temperature) increases the vibrations of the atoms and molecules and causes them to move to points of equilibrium away from the original ones. This produces **expansion** of the solid in all directions. The metal expands more and faster then the enamel, and returns to its original dimensions when it cools. When the enamel piece is removed from the kiln, the metal substrate continues to be incandescent for a longer period than the enamel, which cools faster. Thus, when the enamel is almost cooled but still ductile, it is possible to fix deformations in the support produced by expansion by applying weight (using irons or spatulas) to the piece

---

KILN TEMPERATURES

Today most kilns have a thermometer, but it is helpful to know how to recognize the interior temperature based on the color of the kiln. This allows you to check the temperature range with a quick glance.

Approximate Temperature Range	Color	
From about 1,250 to 1,400°F (680 to 760°C)	Dark cherry red	
From about 1,435 to 1,475°F (780 to 800°C)	Orange red	
From about 1,560 to 1,650°F (850 to 900°C)	Bright yellow orange	
Above about 1,650°F (900°C)	Bright yellow	

BEHAVIOR OF ENAMEL DURING FIRING

1. This is the enamel before firing. The application should be uniform; the surface should be perfectly smooth with an even coating. The enamel should reach all the way to the edges without going past them.

3. The enamel becomes more fluid and particles begin to bond to each other. The spaces between them disappear and the piece begins to shine. The surface tension of the enamel is less than the force of gravity. The result is an enamel piece with a rough surface similar to an orange peel.

2. In the first phase, the enamel shows some changes caused by the temperature. It begins to soften and the viscosity diminishes, although the surface tension is greater than the fluidity. It adheres to the surface of the metal, maintaining its original shape because the particles are touching each other, but without becoming very fluid. This enamel has a granulated texture with spaces between the particles, similar to sugar or frost.

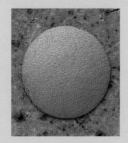

4. In the last phase, the particles are closely joined, the enamel becomes very fluid, and the viscosity is diminished. It has completely melted, and the surface is smooth and shiny. When it cools, the enamel piece looks shiny, polished, and smooth, with its true color.

Effects of Excess Firing

Retraction of the enamel layer from the edges of the piece, where the oxidized metal can be seen (in this case copper). Small, dark bare spots can also be observed.

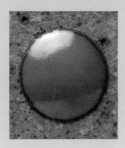

Retraction of the layer and, as a consequence, appearance of the metal. Change in the color of the enamel; for example, the yellow turns green through the effects of oxidation of the copper. If the enamel is in the kiln for a long time, it can disappear or completely transform itself, depending on its hardness and the thickness of the layer.

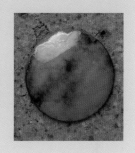

while the metal is still malleable. These differences in expansion and **contraction** of both materials are sometimes responsible for their **incompatibility**, which can cause cracks and other problems with the enamel. This is why it is necessary to control the thickness and layers of enamel.

The choice of metal thickness should be based on the technique that will be used, and on the size and shape of the piece (flat, twisted, curved, or rounded). Also consider whether it needs an undercoat of flux or not, the number of firings required, and the projected number of layers. Practice and experience will help you determine the best thickness for each project.

Enamel Counter Coat

The counter coat helps control the expansion and contraction of the metal, reduces oxidation of the support, and keeps possible oxidized particles from depositing on the surface of the enamel. The counter coat and the layer of enamel on the other side sandwich the metal and remove the expansion–contraction forces, preventing possible deformations in the support, which can cause cracks to appear in the thin, fragile layer of enamel. It is of utmost importance to establish a proper balance between the upper layers of enamel and the counter layer on the underside. It is not necessary to have the same number of layers as long as they maintain a certain proportion. One layer of counter enamel for three on the upper side is recommended.

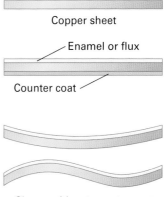

Copper sheet

Enamel or flux

Counter coat

Sheets without counter coat

▲ The sheets with a counter coat conserve their original form, the rest become warped.

Preparation and Cleaning of Enamel

The preparation and cleaning of enamels are fundamental to the art of enameling, and in large part the success of your work depends on them. It is very important to know how to do these steps, since they are the beginning of the entire process.

Grinding

The grinding process is used to improve the enamel particles, adjusting their size according to your requirements and the technical processes that will be used. Nowadays manufacturers can supply different custom grain sizes based on the amount ordered. It is also necessary to grind enamel if it has developed lumps and clumps during storage; this must be done before washing since it will not be effective otherwise. Grinding is not necessary when the particles supplied by the manufacturer meet the requirements of your work.

Grinding is done in a mortar, with a small amount of material at a time. If it is necessary to grind a large amount of enamel, it should be done in phases, grinding and then washing it each time. There are also electric laboratory grinders, which work very well for moderate amounts.

Cleaning

Nowadays the enamels we buy are very clean, thanks to modern manufacturing processes. However, they may contain enamel dust or fines, as well as impurities and other particles from the manufacturing process. Cleaning is an attempt to purify the enamel and prepare it for technical processes. It is most important for transparent enamels since their clarity, transparency, sheen, and color depend on cleanliness. On the other hand, opaque enamels do not require such a deep cleaning and can be cleaned with fewer steps.

The cleaning can be done wet, by rinsing the enamels, or dry, by sifting the particles. Here we show the wet method in detail, as it is the method used in most of the exercises in this book. Only the basic steps of the dry cleaning process are described. It goes without saying that all steps of the cleaning process, and the handling of enamels in general, should take place in a perfectly clean environment with clean utensils.

◄ 1. For hand grinding, a small amount of tap water or distilled water is placed in the mortar (in this case it is made of agate) and then a small amount of enamel is added with a spatula. A rotary motion is made with the pestle held vertically, while applying pressure on the enamel. Continue doing this until you can no longer hear the sound of the friction of the particles, which indicates that the enamel is ground.

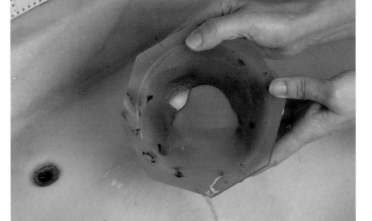

◄ 2. The enamel is left to stand in the mortar and the excess water is decanted. Then the enamel is washed.

PARTICLES

Storing wet enamels for a long period of time can cause particles to become suspended on the surface of the water. The solution is washing again in distilled water. If the results of testing are not good, the enamel can be washed again with the addition of two drops of nitric acid.

Washing

Washing refers to the process of removing dust and impurities—and also the salts produced by the reaction of the enamel to the water—by decanting. Enamel has a chemical reaction with water, which causes an exchange of hydronium ions (H_3O+) from the water with the alkali ions on the enamel. Then, partial hydration occurs in the topmost layers of the silica particles contained in the enamel, which can dissolve. This process can continue over time, increasing the amount of alkali in the solution.

Washing is done in several steps; tap water may be used in all but the last, when distilled water is required. Or, distilled water may be used for all steps, although this is a bit more expensive. It is not always necessary to add drops of nitric acid, as it depends on the brand of the enamel, and it is unnecessary in most cases when using opaque enamels. Acid is not needed for cleaning opaque red, orange, or pink enamels.

After washing, the enamels that will be applied wet are kept in bottles, and those that will be used dry are dried. This is done by placing a small amount of enamel in a wide, flat container (an aluminum tray or glass vessel, for example) or on a piece of aluminum foil in a clean location to allow the water to evaporate. To encourage evaporation, it can be placed under a strong lightbulb or on top of a kiln that is not too hot.

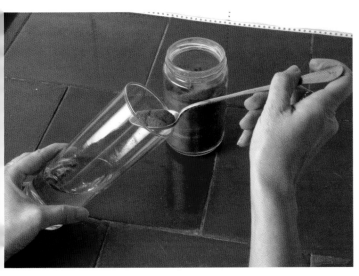

▲ 1. A tall, thin glass is filled about one quarter full with tap water, and no more than two or three spoonfuls of enamel are added. It is important to add the water before the enamel to avoid creating dust and lumps in the water.

▲ 2. Next, it is mixed by gently swirling the water in the glass. Never use a spoon or other instrument, as this can cause the creation of more dust particles.

▼ 3. The glass is filled with water directly from the tap to stir up the particles.

▲ 4. This causes the enamel to become suspended in the water.

▲ 5. It is left to sit until the enamel forms a sediment in the bottom of the glass.

CLOUDINESS

Cloudiness is caused by fines, superfine particles of enamel from the grinding process that are suspended in the water and give it a white, cloudy look. This means that the enamel was not washed well and the powdered enamel is still in it. The solution is another washing.

▲ **6.** The water is removed by decanting, tipping the glass slowly and gently in the sink. The enamel stays in the bottom of the glass. It is filled again with tap water and the process is repeated, allowing the enamel to form sediment, then decanting it.

▲ **7.** Several colors are washed at one time for more efficiency.

◄ **8.** The process of washing with tap water and then decanting is repeated as many times as is necessary until the water is completely clear.

▶ **9.** In the last decanting, when barely a finger's width of water is left covering the enamel, two drops of nitric acid are added to eliminate any possible organic and metallic impurities. The water is then swirled in the glass for 30 seconds.

▶ **10.** The glass is filled with tap water and the process is repeated as before, allowing the sediment to form and decanting the water. This is repeated four or five times, adding tap water each time.

◀ **11.** Finally, distilled water is used four or five times while repeating the decanting process, filling the glass just one quarter full. If it is to be applied wet, the clean enamel can be put in a wide-mouthed container with distilled water; if it is to be applied dry, it is dried and stored in a closed bottle.

Sifting

Another way to clean enamels is by sifting. This is done using standardized screens for separating the particles by their size. The screens generally are 100, 200, and 325 mesh (see page 28), although it is possible to use other sizes according to the particular needs of each project. The enamel is sifted through the screens, and the particles larger than 100 mesh (0.117 mm) stay in the first screen, those larger than 200 mesh (0.074 mm) in the second, and those larger than 325 mesh (0.004 mm) stay in the last, while the smallest particles pass through it. The largest grains are the cleanest, while the finest ones are dirtier and have more fines, or dust-like particles.

◀ Several stacking screens with standard meshes can be used for sifting. They are assembled with the largest mesh (100) on the top, then the 200 mesh and 325 mesh below it in that order, with a tray at the bottom to catch the finest grains. Then the enamel is poured in the top screen.

▶ A lid is placed on the top and the enamel is sifted by gently shaking the sifters from side to side.

STORING ENAMELS IN WATER

Enamels that will be applied wet are covered with distilled water. If the water evaporates, more should not be added, as there may be impurities in the enamel that will affect its transparency or cause bubbles. When enamels have dried out, they must be washed again briefly with distilled water.

The bottles must not be tipped or stored upside down because this will cause enamel deposits on the lid and in the screw top. Jars of enamel with water should not be shaken because this might mix in particles deposited on the lid and the edges of the jar.

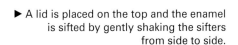

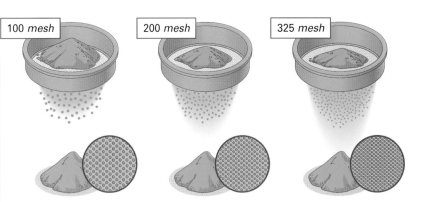

| 100 *mesh* | 200 *mesh* | 325 *mesh* |

▲ The particles larger than 100 mesh are the cleanest, while those that have passed through the 325 mesh are the dirtiest.

Cleaning Metals

It is of utmost importance to clean the metal support before applying enamel to it. Proper adhesion of the enamel to the support depends on this, and it will influence the quality and look of the final piece. Oils, particles, dirt, and oxides deposited on the surface of the metal can affect the colors, especially the clarity of transparent enamels. The cleaning process should be done immediately before the enamel is applied, otherwise the metal can oxidize again or become dirty. Cleaning means eliminating grease and oxides from the metal and, if required, polishing, which is important when using transparent enamels. We will look at two methods of cleaning copper.

Cleaning with Acid

Cleaning with acid degreases and strips the metal while helping to polish it, and for this reason it is recommended for those working with transparent enamels. The process must take place in a space with a hood and exhaust fan, and protective gear (nitrile gloves, tongs, safety glasses, and proper clothing) must be used. In addition, used acid must be disposed of according to the published guidelines. The cleaning happens in a tub, filled first with water before the acid is added, never the other way around.

◀ 1. First, the copper support is annealed in the kiln until it turns dark cherry red. After it is removed, a layer of cupric oxide (calamina) appears as the metal cools. This is later removed by rinsing the piece under a running tap.

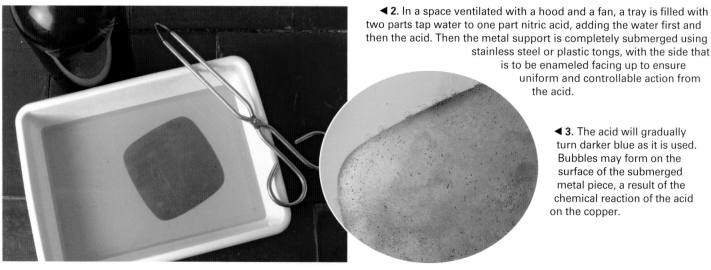

◀ 2. In a space ventilated with a hood and a fan, a tray is filled with two parts tap water to one part nitric acid, adding the water first and then the acid. Then the metal support is completely submerged using stainless steel or plastic tongs, with the side that is to be enameled facing up to ensure uniform and controllable action from the acid.

◀ 3. The acid will gradually turn darker blue as it is used. Bubbles may form on the surface of the submerged metal piece, a result of the chemical reaction of the acid on the copper.

▲ 4. The bubbles must be removed to ensure uniform action of the acid; this is done with a bird feather. When the metal shows an even pink tone, it can be removed with the tongs and rinsed with plenty of running water.

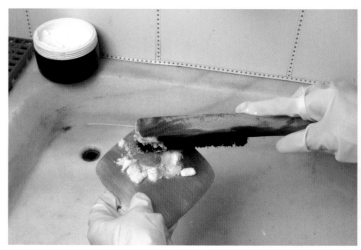

▲ 5. While wearing nitrile gloves, scrub the metal with bicarbonate and water using a natural bristle brush to neutralize the acid. Finally, rinse it with running water and dry it with a clean rag, holding it along the edges so that no oils will be deposited on the surface.

Cleaning with Vinegar

An alternative to acid is cleaning with salt and vinegar. Although it is a bit slower because it requires more immersion time, it is safer for people and the environment. After cleaning, the support must be handled carefully, holding it by the edges so that your fingers don't leave residual oils.

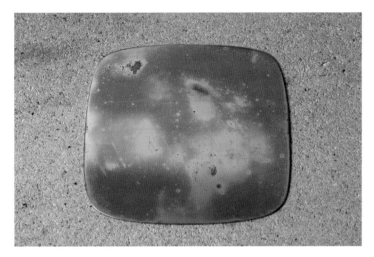

◄ **1.** First, the support is annealed in the kiln at a very low temperature until it has a reddish tone; then it is allowed to cool. It is not necessary to wait for calamine to form as in the acid method.

PROBLEM: INSUFFICIENT CLEANING

Insufficient cleaning of the support can lead to problems. Here, the copper support oxidized during firing, and began to flake in places, and the enamel receded in these places, pulling the calamine with it.

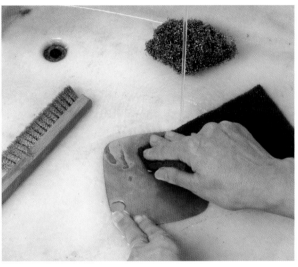

◄ **2.** Salt is added to a container of vinegar until it reaches the saturation point, and then the support is submerged in the mixture. This method is slower than using acid, so the support must be left in the bath for a longer period of time. It is taken out and rinsed with lots of running water, rubbing the surface with a scrubbing pad and a wire brush to remove all traces of oxidation. Next, it is scrubbed with a bristle brush and bicarbonate with water to remove grease and vinegar, rinsed, and allowed to dry.

CLEANING PRECIOUS METALS		
Pure Metals		After they are annealed, they are allowed to cool. The metal does not oxidize, so enamel can be applied immediately. They must be handled carefully because touching them with your fingers will leave oils.
Metal Alloys	Gold and Sterling Silver	Moderate annealing. Clean in an acid bath of sulphuric or nitric acid in various proportions: 75% water and 25% acid for slow, gentle pickling that is less aggressive and noxious, or 50% water and 50% acid for a fast, more aggressive cleaning that will create more fumes than the other approach. Heating the bath will accelerate the processes. The metal is removed from the bath when the black oxide disappears (a product of the copper used in the alloy). Rinse under running water while scrubbing with bicarbonate to neutralize any remaining acids. In the corners and in case of resistant oxidation, it can be scrubbed with a fiberglass or wire brush until those areas are clean. Rinse again with running water and dry with a clean rag.
	Gold and Sterling Silver Plate	Pieces manufactured using an electroplating process and subsequent special treatments for polishing, may show up at the enameling studio with encrusted impurities. They must be cleaned in an acid bath. They can also be boiled in tap water to remove impurities, polishing compound, wax, grease, and so on. It is also possible to use an ultrasonic cleaner, which can be very practical and effective.
Jewelry Pieces in Alloys (second or third phase of enameling)	Gold and Sterling Silver	Acids can damage the surface of fired enamelware. In jewelrymaking the work is usually carried out in phases, so between firings certain areas can be submerged or painted with hydrofluoric acid to dissolve the copper oxide (present in the alloy) on the surface, avoiding the areas that have already been enameled. This works better when hot, but it can be quite dangerous if you do not take proper precautions and use protective gear. Rinse, neutralize, and dry without touching with your hands.

Applying Enamel

Enamel can be applied to a cleaned and prepared metal support using two different methods: wet application or dry application. Both techniques are good, but each has particular aspects that make it better for some uses.

Wet Application

Applying wet, or wet packing, is done using enamel that is mixed with distilled water as an agglutinate, an agent that maintains the cohesion of the particles that are applied to the support. Generally, wet application requires some skill and practice, and it works well for creating small pieces with a lot of detail, which require precision. The application should be as uniform and homogenous as possible, so that the grains are very close together and the layer is approximately 0.04 in (1 mm) thick. It is very important to control the amount of water in the enamel to avoid problems. Excess water will cause the enamel to run and pull the enamel away, which will cause areas of oxidation to appear later. You must proceed carefully so that the grains stay in contact with each other, well packed and applied right up to the edges of the support without going over them. The first layer cannot be done halfway because the support will oxidize and the enamel that is already applied will dry out, causing muddy areas if you go back to add more water to the layer.

Wet packing can be done with a brush or spatula, but the latter is better for working with large surfaces and certain techniques. To begin the enameling process, a counter coat is applied to the back of the support; then a layer of flux or other enamel is applied to the other side and the first firing is done. Successive layers of enamel can then be applied.

▲ 1. Before starting, a tray is placed on the table with two sticks on top of it to hold the support (in this case it is copper) with the backside facing up, so it can be covered with a counter coat. The piece is held at the edges to keep from depositing oils on the surface with the fingers, and a layer of methylcellulose glue is applied.

▲ 2. The counter coat is applied working from the outside in. A small amount of the enamel is picked up with the brush and deposited on the support by dabbing it. Make sure the particles stay in contact with the metal and that you spread an even coat over the substrate.

ERRORS IN APPLICATION

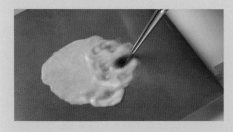

The layer should be uniform and homogenous, and the enamel applied carefully so that the particles are always in contact with each other. Do not leave areas with a greater thickness or areas without enamel.

Do not charge the brush with too much enamel.

▲ 3. The coat is applied from the outside in, following the edges and making a concentric shape that ends in the center of the piece.

◄ **4.** The spatula is used just like the brush to deposit small amounts of enamel. In this case, it is very important to use just the right amount of water to avoid problems; the enamel should have a texture similar to the beach sand used to construct sand castles. To keep the support from moving during the application, it can be held with a burnishing tool or another spatula. When the application is finished, blotter paper is gently laid over the piece without applying pressure to absorb excess water (see pages 72–73).

▼ **5.** The next step is applying flux to the back of the support. If the piece is domed, start at the highest point and work toward the edges. Distilled water should be used to moisten the brush after each application. A clean cotton or linen rag can be used to remove excess water, if required, but it should be used very carefully near the enamel.

▼ **6.** In convex pieces the enamel is first applied to the center (the highest point), and subsequent applications should follow a concentric pattern as they move toward the outside. It is done this way so that the water will not drip on the enamel or accumulate at the edges of the support. Then it is applied to the corners, from inside to outside, being careful at the edges.

► **7.** When the application is finished, it is allowed to dry by evaporation and then immediately fired before the support can begin to oxidize.

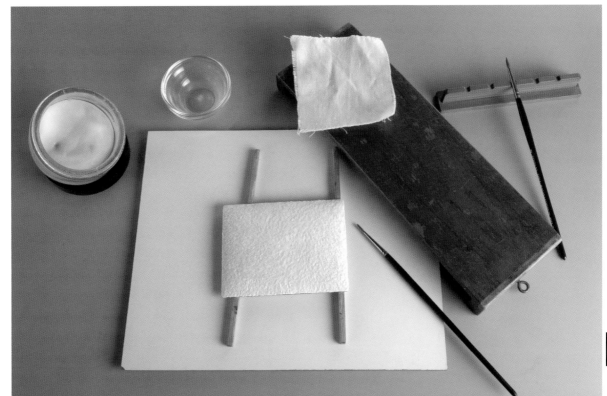

Dry Application

Dry application, or dusting, takes place without the use of any agglutinate in the enamel. The enamel is applied to the support by sifting. This is a quick way to apply enamel, and very useful for large pieces and large areas. However, it does not allow the creation of fine details like wet enamel does, and it uses more enamel material. It is very good for working with stencils and for blending, shading, and creating color effects. It can make very uniform layers; even on supports with inclined edges you can use glue to make the enamel adhere.

The enamel is applied by sifting it through a mesh. The mesh is held 4 in (10 cm) above the support and spread over the entire surface while lightly tapping the screen to make it fall through. This operation does not require the skill that wet application does, but it takes some practice to be able to create a uniform layer. A dust mask should be worn to avoid inhaling particles of enamel.

◄ **1.** The counter coat is applied to the back first. The metal support is placed on a sheet of paper or cardboard on top of the worktable, which will allow you to recover the extra enamel, and a layer of methylcellulose glue is applied. Then the mesh is filled with dry enamel, held 4 in (10 cm) above the support, and tapped lightly to make it fall over the surface.

► **2.** It is sprayed with distilled water to activate the glue and adhere the enamel. This should be done from a careful distance, about 20 in (50 cm), depending on the sprayer, making sure that the water does not drip and create pits and trenches in the enamel.

◄ **3.** The piece is immediately put on a tray with two sticks to hold it up, and the water is removed with a piece of blotter paper cut slightly larger than the support.

▼ **4.** The blotter paper is placed over the piece without applying pressure. It only touches the edges of the piece and absorbs the water through osmosis, leaving all the enamel slightly moist. This allows the piece to be turned over without the enamel that is adhered to the glue falling off.

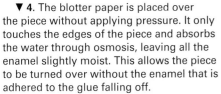

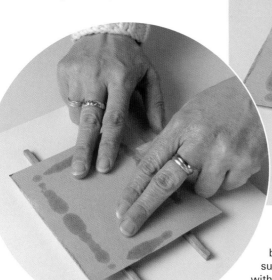

▲ **5.** Here is the finished counter coat. Flux is applied in the same way, but without applying the methylcellulose glue. The entire process is done dry, without using water because it could affect the transparency of the enamel by encouraging oxidation on the support. On pieces that are very curved or of large dimensions, water can be applied with a sprayer to ensure adhesion of the enamel, but it may affect its transparency. It is also possible to apply glue, which should be very purified, with special aerosols (see page 126 and the following).

Firing and Final Results

After the counter coat or the flux has been applied, the firing phase begins. The piece should be completely dry, since any water contained in the enamel will boil, creating bubbles and causing the enamel to separate from the metal. The planche should already be in the kiln (previously turned on and brought to working temperature), and removed hot. The piece is placed on the planche using a wide spatula, with the side with the flux up and the counter coat in contact with the planche. Then it is placed in the kiln, already heated to 1,650°F (900°C), and the piece is fired (see pages 61–62). The result should be a shiny, uniform counter coat and a transparent, smooth, and shiny flux coat ready to receive the next layers.

◀ **1.** The first step is to prepare the planche. This one is made of ceramic fibers. A coat of kaolin mixed with water is applied to both sides and allowed to dry.

◀ **2.** The enamel piece is placed on the planche using the wide spatula, and the planche is put into the kiln.

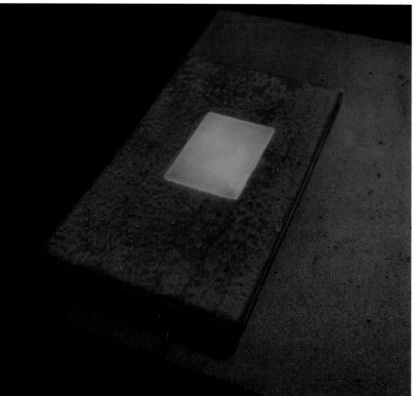

◀ **3.** The piece is observed during the process, and it is removed from the kiln when its surface is smooth and shiny. The enamel is still soft when the piece is removed from the kiln, and it should be kept in a perfectly clean place until it has cooled completely so that no particles of dust can adhere to it. Refractory supports are best for firing since they preserve the temperature for a longer time and keep the enamel from suffering thermal shock while it is cooling.

FLUX

Flux absorbs the copper oxide that is created during firing. If there is excessive heat, it will cause the appearance of greenish tones because more oxide is created than can be absorbed by the flux. If, on the other hand, there is not enough heat, reddish tones will appear in some areas of the flux because of oxides that still have not been absorbed.

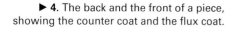

▶ **4.** The back and the front of a piece, showing the counter coat and the flux coat.

SOLVING PROBLEMS: HOLES IN THE ENAMEL

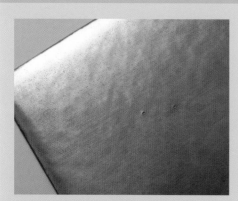

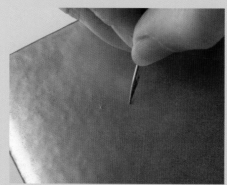

The appearance of tiny holes where the underlying metal shows through after firing can be attributed to defects in the application of the enamel (an application that is irregular or too thin), enamel that was still moist, or excessive firing.

The solution for this problem is a mechanical cleaning of the holes with a steel point, or a chemical cleaning with a drop of nitric acid, later cleaning with water and bicarbonate, and rinsing with distilled water.

Next a new layer of flux is applied to the holes and the piece is fired for a shorter time than before. Unfortunately, the mark left by repairing the defect will be somewhat visible in some cases.

Palettes and samples of enamels are a necessity in the studio. They must be made before any pieces are created, and great care should be taken with them since they will be the guides for later work. When they are finished, you will keep them in the studio as references for later projects. They will be very helpful for working efficiently, saving you time and helping avoid errors and defects. They are indispensable for understanding the behavior of enamels and how they react with each other and with the metals and supports, and also for establishing a range of hardness. The colors of enamels change when they are fired, and they also differ depending on the kind of metal of the support, whether they are applied directly to the metal or separated from it by a layer of flux, the thickness of the application, and how they are layered. Palettes are not used only for enamel; they also must be created for vitreous paints to illustrate how they react. The requirements of the project will dictate how the palettes are created, whether very simple applications of enamel or paint or complex affairs with several layers, different foils, and base coats. A reference label should be added next to each enamel or paint, or on the back of the palette or sample, so it can be identified.

Transparent Enamel Palettes

Transparent enamel palettes are usually 0.125-in thick (0.3 mm) metal sheets that are prepared by marking different areas with a metal scribe and then cleaning before applying the base coat. It is a somewhat laborious process that requires several applications and at least four firings; however, the time spent on this task will be worth the effort for the creation of future works of art. Now we will show you how to create a palette.

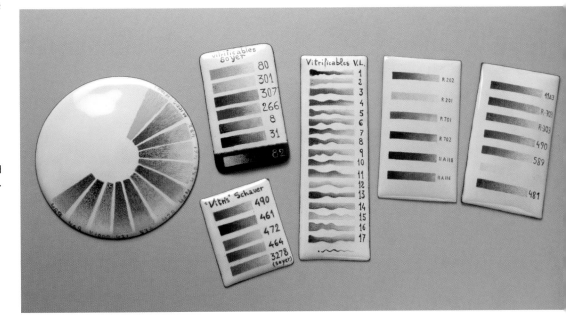

▶ Samples of vitreous paints applied over opaque white enamel.

▼ A set of transparent enamel palettes.

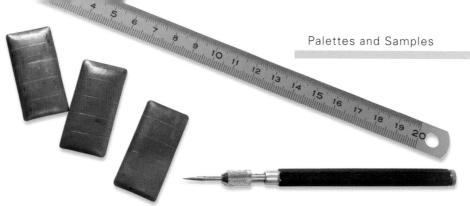

◀ The areas for the different applications are marked on the palette with a steel scribe; then it is cleaned and a counter coat is applied.

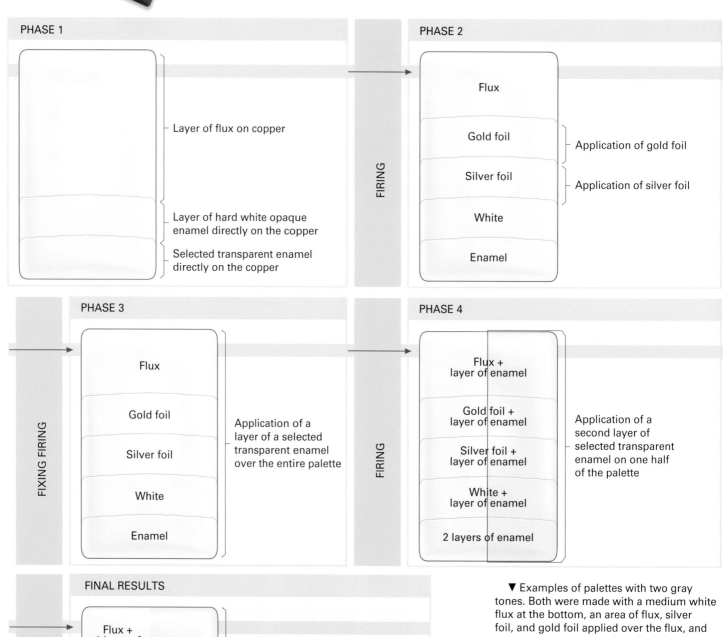

PHASE 1

- Layer of flux on copper

- Layer of hard white opaque enamel directly on the copper
- Selected transparent enamel directly on the copper

FIRING

PHASE 2

Flux

Gold foil — Application of gold foil

Silver foil — Application of silver foil

White

Enamel

FIXING FIRING

PHASE 3

Flux

Gold foil

Silver foil

White

Enamel

Application of a layer of a selected transparent enamel over the entire palette

FIRING

PHASE 4

Flux + layer of enamel

Gold foil + layer of enamel

Silver foil + layer of enamel

White + layer of enamel

2 layers of enamel

Application of a second layer of selected transparent enamel on one half of the palette

FINAL RESULTS

FIRING

Flux + 1 layer of enamel — Two layers of selected transparent enamel over flux on copper

Gold foil + 1 layer of enamel — Two layers of selected transparent enamel over gold foil

Silver foil + 1 layer of enamel — Two layers of selected transparent enamel over silver foil

White + 1 layer of enamel — Two layers of selected transparent enamel over hard opaque white

2 layers of enamel — Three layers of selected transparent enamel directly over copper

▼ Examples of palettes with two gray tones. Both were made with a medium white flux at the bottom, an area of flux, silver foil, and gold foil applied over the flux, and transparent gray enamel applied directly on the copper support. Then a layer of gray enamel was applied to the entire palette and another layer of the same was applied vertically on the right side.

Opaque Palettes

Palettes of opaque enamels are simpler than those of transparent colors. After the support is cleaned and a counter coat applied, a first coat of enamel is applied to the palette and fired. Generally a second layer is added to one half of the palette and fired again. The resulting palette is an example of one and two coats of enamel.

Hardness Palettes

Hardness palettes are made with different colors from the same or different ranges. They indicate the behavior of the rest of the colors in respect to a single reference color during firing. Generally, after the support is prepared (cleaned and counter coat applied) the first phase begins: a reference enamel—for example, a medium or soft opaque white—is applied directly to the support in one area and a flux base coat is applied to the rest of the palette and then fired. In the second phase, selected colors are applied over the flux and it is fired again. In the last phase, a second layer of each color is applied over

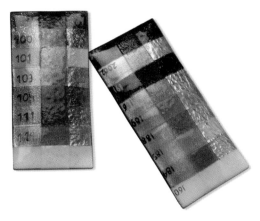

▲ Samples and palette with opalescent enamels.

▲ Examples of hardness palettes. Both were fired in the first phase with an area of medium opaque white enamel (at the bottom) applied directly to the support, and flux on the rest of the palette. In the second phase, silver foil was applied vertically on the right side and then fired. In the next phase, horizontal samples of different transparent colors were added and fired. Finally, a second layer was applied over each color, including the white reference color, in the center part of the palette, creating a vertical strip with a double layer where the hardness of the different colors can be appreciated.

one half of each, including the reference color. During the final firing, the changes in the reference color are observed and the palette is removed from the kiln when the metal looks like it is at the fusion point. The colors that have a rough or granular surface are harder than the reference enamel. This can also be done by juxtaposing opaque enamels, using white as a reference.

▼ Samples of opaque enamels.

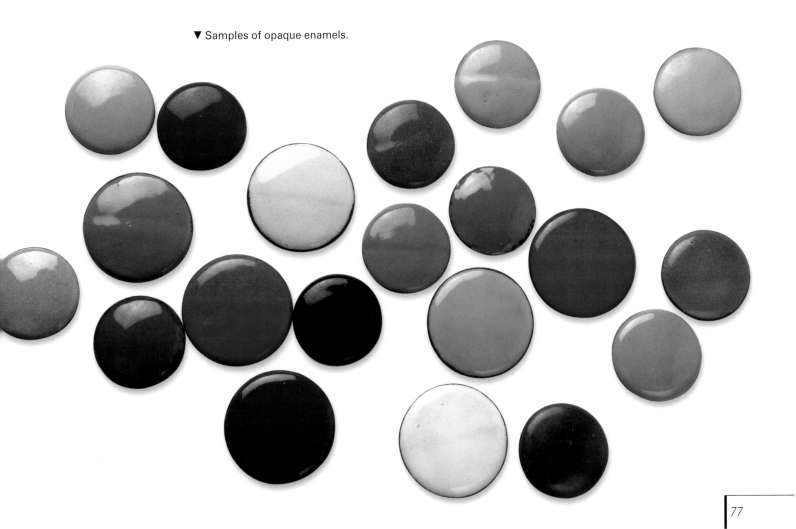

*O*nce the basic theory and the preliminary processes involved in enameling are understood, we can approach the different techniques on solid ground. In the following pages we will explain the different techniques of enamel art, showing in detail the different methods and processes involved.

Painted Enamel

The term painted enamel includes the various techniques that can be used to create works with painting-like results. Although it is not a very accurate term, it has been widely accepted by the international community. In these techniques, the enamel is applied by juxtaposing and superimposing different layers until an image is created, the same way a painter would work on a canvas.

In the following pages, we will show the different techniques grouped according to the application method used, whether wet (painted enamel and grisaille) or dry. First, the preliminary steps are explained, which include preparing of the support and transferring the images to it. Then, we will cover the first technique, which consists of applying foil to the work. The metal thickness required depends on the size of each piece and on whether it will have counter enamel or not. Generally, for pieces smaller than 3 inches (8 cm), we recommend a thickness of 0.008 to 0.010 in (0.2 to 0.3 mm); for medium pieces, 4 to 10 in (10 to 25 cm), a thickness of 0.02 to 0.024 in (0.5 to 0.6 mm); for larger pieces, a thickness of 0.028 to 0.040 in (0.7 to 1.0 mm), and for pieces without counter enamel, from 0.040 to 0.060 in (1.0 to 1.5 mm). Whether counter enamel is used or not

◄ Andreu Vilasís (Barcelona, Spain). *Venècia*, 2004. Painted enamel and gold and silver foils. 6 × 6 in (15 × 15 cm).

will be dictated by the work planned for the front, but generally the use of counter enamel is recommended.

Preliminary Work: Preparation and Copying

Once the support is clean and ready (see pages 68–69) and has been fired, it has to be prepared before the enamel is applied. The outside edges of the copper support oxidize with each firing, which creates a fairly wide oxidized line when the piece cools down. If

this line is not eliminated, particles of copper oxide (calamina) could dislodge during the firing process and adhere to the layer of enamel that is being fired, causing black points or spots. To avoid this, the oxidized particles are cleaned with a wet carborundum bar and dried afterward. This process (called stoning or cleaning the edges) should be performed with all the techniques between the various firing steps while the piece is cold, before touching up or applying the next layer. It can also be used to remove excess enamel from the edges of the piece or enamel that

STONING

In enameling, the removal of enamel by mechanical means is called stoning. This process is carried out wet, with a bar of carborundum, or with an electric lapping or grinding machine. Stoning eliminates the imperfections that result during firing, such as stains or dark and rough areas; it can also be used to smooth out a layer of enamel or to remove it completely. For the latter, the piece is placed flat on the work surface over a clean rag. Then, the piece is held firmly with one hand while rubbing the problem area vigorously with the carborundum bar, consistently and without applying too much pressure, wetting it often. It is rinsed under running water to check the results. The process is repeated as often as needed until the problem area or the layer in question is eliminated. Finally, it is washed with ammonia and water, dried with a clean rag, and fired to restore the shininess to the surface.

◄ **1.** The oxidation from the edges is eliminated by grinding. The piece is rubbed with a bar of carborundum under running water, moving it up and down from the enameled side (top of the piece) to the side with the base coat (back of the piece).

extends beyond the edges of the support, a point to keep in mind if the pieces are to be framed or mounted on jewelry afterward.

Transfer paper can be used to transfer the motif onto the flux surface. The transfer method does not differ from any other transfer method; the lines of the drawing that will serve as guides for the application of the enamel will bind to the piece after firing. This phase requires attention and some practice to be able to establish the appropriate length of time needed. In general, white transfer paper is used on transparent and opaque enamel colors, while graphite or tracing paper is used on light opaque enamels. The enamel is applied right after the design is transferred, on both sides, since the graphite will disappear after the first firing.

▶ **2.** To trace the design on the flux support, the first step is to transfer the main forms of the design onto tracing paper. To do this, the borders of the piece are established and the angles marked.

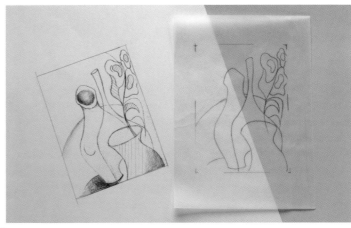

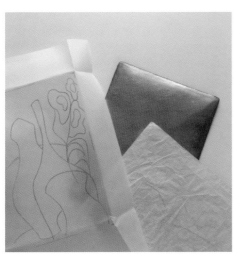

◀ **3.** The tracing paper is placed over the support, making sure that the sides and corners fit over it. By doing this, we make sure that the design is perfectly centered and that the tracing paper will fit properly later.

▶ **4.** After removing the tracing paper, the white transfer paper is placed over the support, with the self-copying side in contact with the flux. Then, the tracing paper is folded around it, now perfectly centered.

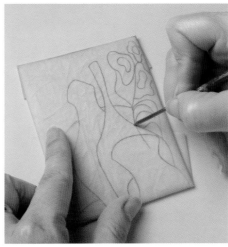

◀ **5.** The forms are transferred by tracing the lines with a round-tipped metal tool, without applying too much pressure. It is important to proceed carefully to avoid missing some areas or going over others more than once.

◀ **6.** The design is transferred onto the flux coated support. It is made permanent by firing, and will require a shorter firing time than the enamel. Monitor the transfer paper during the process. The binder contained in the paper will burn off, but the pigments will remain and adhere to the layer of flux. Once the binder burns off, the transfer paper becomes white. It is left to rest for a moment before it is pulled out of the kiln. If left in too long, the transfer disappears and the process has to be repeated.

◀ **7.** To make sure that the tracing has properly bonded to the support, go over one of the design's side or bottom lines carefully with the tip of the spatula. If the line disappears, the procedure has to be repeated.

Applying and Working with Foils

One approach to working with painted enamels is the application of foils. Gold or silver foils are applied to enamel surfaces that have already been fired (here, over the flux base) and that are covered with a new layer of transparent enamel. Some transparent enamels can change colors when they come into contact with the metal (see page 26). To counter this effect, it is necessary to apply a specific type of flux (one for each metal) over the foil, firing it before the colored enamel is applied. Foils create a luminous effect thanks to the reflection of light on their surface, which bounces back through the enamel and changes colors.

Foils are bonded to the lower layer of enamel by a brief firing. It is important to monitor the behavior of the foil. Insufficient firing time can prevent the foil from adhering to the enamel properly, causing it to dislodge and roll back during the next firing step, which will remove the top layer of enamel. On the other hand, excessive firing time can take away their shiny appearance and cause foils to break or even disappear. This phenomenon can be used to create textured effects. If the foils turn out too wrinkled, this could be due to the fact that the underlying enamel is wrinkled as well, or that the glue used on them was applied incorrectly or did not evaporate properly.

Finally, the upper layer of enamel should be applied thinly and evenly; it can cause problems if applied any other way. On the other hand, the firing time of applied decals and foils is so brief that the appearance of calamina, and thus oxidation, is kept to a minimum, and therefore there is no need for removal.

▲ Núria L. Ribalta (Barcelona, Spain). Paperweight, 2004. Painted enamel and silver and gold foils over copper. 3½ in (9 cm) in diameter.

▲ ▶ **1.** The foil is placed completely flat inside a piece of very fine sandpaper (in this case number 400), and is folded in half like a book. The surface is rubbed by pressing with the thumbnail. This provides a wide, rounded surface that will prevent lines from forming.

▲ **2.** The result is the appearance of small holes in the foil, which are visible when held against the light. These pores allow vapors to escape during the firing process, preventing the foil from bubbling up or wrinkling because of the air or water pockets in the glue trapped underneath. They also facilitate the foil's adhesion to the layers of enamel above and below.

▲ **3.** Foils are extremely thin and cannot be cut directly. They should be placed inside a sheet of tracing paper folded in half like a book. A rectangular piece of tracing paper, somewhat larger than the design, is cut off and the design is traced with a pencil.

►► **4.** The paper with the design is folded in half like a book. A piece of the foil is placed inside using tweezers and is cut out with small, very sharp scissors. In this case, since the shape is rounded, we use curved scissors. To cut out straight lines, a craft knife can be used.

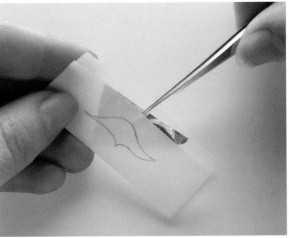

► **5.** Tragacanth gum is applied over the flux in the area designated for the foil. Next, the foil is applied with a brush, picking it up and placing it as desired.

▼ **6.** The foil should stay in place, completely flat. To achieve this, the surface of the foil is gently brushed until the piece looks perfectly flat.

◄ **7.** The rest of the foil cutouts are applied. Adjustments can be made when the glue is still wet, but once it dries, the glue will first have to be moistened with distilled water applied with a brush.

81

▲ 8. The foils are bonded with a brief firing, approximately half the time used for a normal layer of enamel but enough for the enamel to soften and for the foil to adhere. It is important to monitor the piece in the kiln to watch when the color appears; when the color changes overall, it is pulled out of the kiln. It is also important to observe the behavior of the tragacanth glue, which upon firing turns black and then vanishes. Once this takes place, the piece is left to rest for about ten additional seconds in the kiln, and then it is taken out. However, practice is the best guide, and it is always preferable to err on the side of deficiency rather than excess. If the foil has not adhered completely, it can be fired a second time. Once the piece is taken out and while it is cooling off, pressure is applied with a spatula or a pad to flatten the foils and help them adhere.

▲ 9. The pad should be made of perfectly clean cotton or linen fibers, never synthetic. Synthetics burn easily and could leave residue stuck to the enamel. (Cotton only gets scorched but does not leave marks.)

PROBLEMS

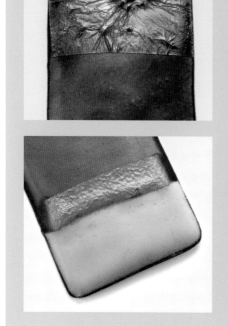

The appearance of bubbles can be caused by inadequate evaporation beneath the foil. If the foil is not properly prepared (sanded to create pores), air or water from the glue can become trapped between the metal and the lower layer of enamel.

Excessive firing can cause the foil to retract and wrinkle too much; in extreme cases, it can even disappear.

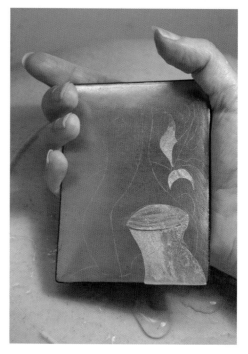

◀ 10. Foils can be manipulated to create specific effects, as in this case, where we rub them with a thin carborundum bar under running water to eliminate certain areas. It is also possible to wrinkle them; to do this, place them between two sheets of tissue paper to produce different textures before they are applied.

◀ 11. We worked on the area inside the vase according to the original design.

Colored Enamel: Wet Application

Enamels can be worked like painting by applying layers. However, there is a difference: With enamels, different colors and tones cannot be created by mixing them because the particles maintain their original color and do not blend with each other once the enamel has been fired. But, when enamels are combined, interesting variations can occur because the particles maintain their original color, producing a pointillism effect. This effect is almost unnoticeable when the enamels are very fine. Color and tonal variations can be achieved by superimposing layers, which should be even and smooth, and applied in order, always maintaining contact between the enamels to make sure that they stay moist. It is important to plan the work and establish the number of firing sessions needed because each one of them constitutes a very critical step. An inadequate final firing can ruin work that was otherwise well executed.

◄ 1. The project is rendered in color, in this case with pencils, which mimic the transparency of the enamel. Watercolors and pastels produce a similar effect.

▼ 2. With the sketch as a guide, we begin applying the enamels (see page 71). We begin in the center and continue outward to better control the moisture. A thin, even layer is applied, rinsing the brush in distilled water thoroughly every time the color is changed.

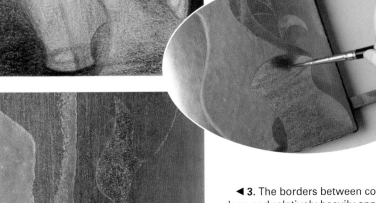

◄ 3. The borders between colors should be clean and relatively heavily applied, creating a sort of wall. The purple color is applied by extending it slightly beyond the foil to create a dark line, as if it were the edge of the first color. Besides creating a drawing effect, it is a good idea to go beyond the foil because the enamel tends to shrink a little during the firing phase, as the surface of the metal is slick.

▼ 4. The rest of the enamels are applied following the sketch. It is a good idea to work with a variety of colors, rinsing the brush in clean water each time the color is changed. Notice the placement of the jars of enamel, in a fan-like arrangement in front of the project, organized so that one side is always covered with water and the other not. The enamel is picked up from the side that is not covered with water, and then the artist can decide how much water is needed.

▼ 5. The first finished layer. It is applied all the way up to the edges of the support. It is left to dry by evaporation, over a heat source (an oven, for example) or under a strong light.

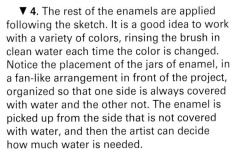

▲ **6.** Since the object will be fired five times in this case, with additional fixative for the foils and the carbon paper, a brief firing is conducted until the enamel acquires the texture of orange peel. Once cooled off, the oxidation from the edges is removed. This process is repeated after each firing.

▲ ▲ **7.** Gold foil pieces are applied as the center of the flowers, like a button, and they are fixed by firing. In some cases, they may appear somewhat darkened after firing.

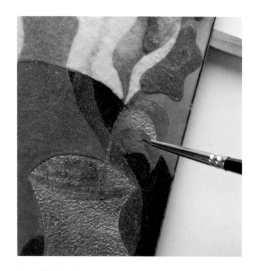

◄ ◄ **8.** A second layer of enamel is applied, which will serve to reinforce the color and to cover the base of the composition and the silver and gold foils.

◄ **9.** Once the second layer is finished, the enamel is left to dry by evaporation. The dry enamel looks opaque.

► **10.** The piece is fired a second time. Then, the design of the bottle in the mid-ground of the composition is copied following the previously explained method, along with the vase and the upper part of the stem with flowers. They are fixed.

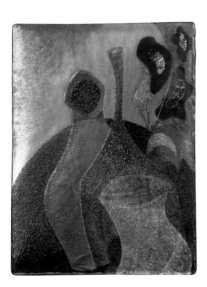

◄ **11.** The third layer of enamel is applied, which will be used to model the long neck of the bottle in the foreground and the wide-mouthed vase in the background, and to touch up the flowers, leaves, and background of the composition—in this case with a gradation, which will help create volume.

► **12.** The piece is fired a third time. We monitor it until it also acquires the texture of an orange peel, almost like a sugar coating, to avoid distressing the first layers too much.

▼ **13.** After that, a fourth layer of enamel is applied to continue forming the background of the composition and the designs of the bottle, the vase, and the flowers. The piece is fired one more time until the surface of the enamel turns smooth and even.

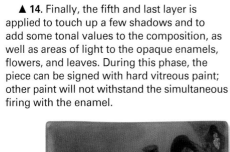

▲ **14.** Finally, the fifth and last layer is applied to touch up a few shadows and to add some tonal values to the composition, as well as areas of light to the opaque enamels, flowers, and leaves. During this phase, the piece can be signed with hard vitreous paint; other paint will not withstand the simultaneous firing with the enamel.

▲ **15.** The piece is placed on a support that has been taken out of the kiln at working temperature, and is then put inside with the help of a firing spatula. The firing process is shorter than the previous one to prevent the vitreous paint from disappearing.

► **16.** The finished piece.

Painted Enamel: Grisaille

Grisaille is a technique that consists of applying monochromatic enamel over a dark background. Various layers are applied until a chiaroscuro effect that has the look of relief modeling is achieved. It can be done with white translucent enamels, or even with opaque ivory or rose over dark brown, violet, blue, green, or dark red. The chiaroscuro effect is created by thickening the enamel in successive layers, producing a very subtle basse-taille look. So, the greater the thickness (greater amount of material) the lighter the color, which will contrast with the thinner areas, whose transparency lets the dark color of the background come through, producing a wide array of medium tonal gradations. Historically, grisaille was produced with Limoges white, but since this material was not readily available and the work involved was extensive, it was used less and less after the last third of the nineteenth century. Opal grisaille has recently been developed.

Opal Grisaille

Opal grisaille involves the use of opalescent enamels (generally white in color) over a dark background executed with transparent enamel. This technique is the result of research conducted by Andreu Vilasís, who used materials other than Limoges white to achieve results similar to traditional grisaille. In this new grisaille, distilled water is used as a vehicle instead of oil essences; this makes the application method and the work process similar to those of all the enamels, in contrast to the traditional grisaille method with Limoges white. Opal grisaille permits the creation of a variety of transparencies and a wide spectrum of chiaroscuro effects, and is appropriate for working with large surfaces. It also has fewer firing risks than grisaille with Limoges white. Updating the traditional technique by using different materials makes it possible to create pieces with fewer technical restrictions, and facilitates freer, more innovative design approaches. Here, Andreu Vilasís demonstrates how to create an opal grisaille piece.

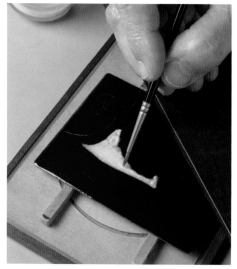

▲ ▶ **2.** Opalescent white enamel (ground in an agate mortar for a more precise application) is applied with the brush over the area that will be thicker—that is, the part that will be lighter (white) when the piece is finished. The enamel is spread evenly with a metal tip.

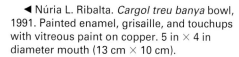

◀ Núria L. Ribalta. *Cargol treu banya* bowl, 1991. Painted enamel, grisaille, and touchups with vitreous paint on copper. 5 in × 4 in diameter mouth (13 cm × 10 cm).

▼ Detail of grisaille work.

◀ ▲ **1.** We draw the original design with pencil on paper. Next, it is transferred onto tissue paper and then copied onto the support, which in this case is covered with a layer of transparent cobalt blue enamel applied directly, without flux.

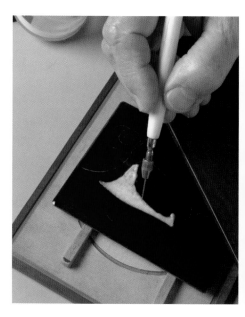

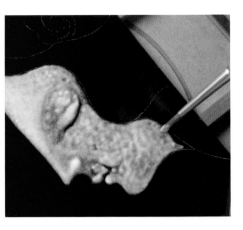

◄ **3.** More enamel is applied in the areas that we want to look lighter: the forehead, the nostrils, the lips, and the eyelid.

▶ **4.** We spread and redistribute the enamel surface with the metal tip. Gradations are created to define the oval shape of the face, the line of the nose, the eyebrow, and the upper lip. The main volumes of the face are defined as if it were a drawing, while the enamel is modeled as if it were a shallow relief.

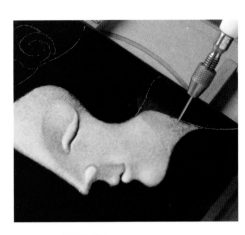

▶ **5.** Enamel is applied area by area to the facial details that need to appear lighter. Notice how the enamel is thicker over the nostril, the eyelid, and the lip.

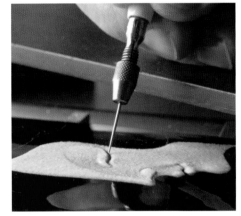

◄ **6.** With the metal tip, we finish defining the forms of the eyes and the lips while the enamel is still slightly wet, which is extremely important if we wish to manipulate it.

◄▶ **7.** Notice the modeling of the layer of enamel and its different thicknesses. The areas that will appear lighter will have more relief than the ones that will be darker. The enamel is left to dry and then fired for the first time.

▶ **8.** After the first firing, we can see that the areas with thicker enamel are lighter, while the ones with a thinner layer appear darker; the blue background shows through thanks to the transparency of the enamel.

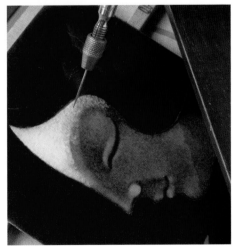

◄ **9.** A second layer of enamel is applied and worked according to the method described, highlighting the shadows that define the face.

▶ **10.** We proceed with the second firing. The result is the finished face. The areas with the most relief appear lighter in tone than the ones with less relief.

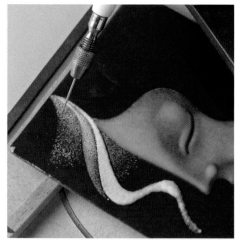

◀ **11.** We continue with the strand of hair over the forehead. We work in an orderly fashion, from the top down, distributing the enamel with the metal tip to create an extremely thin layer on the sides of the strand. The piece is fired for the third time.

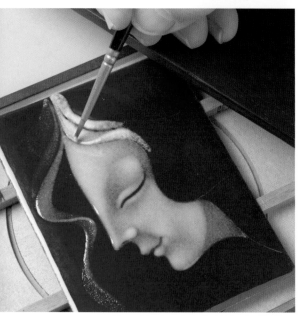

◀▶ **12.** Notice the subtle tonal gradations of the hair strand, from very white areas in the center that emphasize its waviness, to areas where the layer is almost unnoticeable. The enamel for the rest of the hair is applied, with a thicker layer in certain areas to denote waviness; individual strands are also marked by distributing the enamel with the metal point.

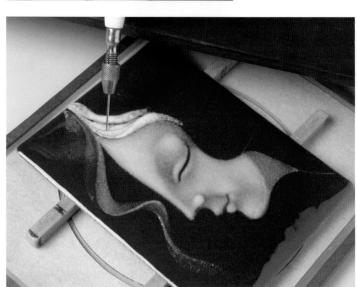

▼ **14.** The piece is fired for the fourth time. The face, made with two layers of enamel, has a lighter tone that contrasts with the hair, which has been made with a single layer of enamel and creates a variety of tonal gradations. Each time the piece is fired, the opal becomes whiter. The final piece is the result of a combination of layers, thicknesses, and firing sessions.

▼ **15.** The layer of enamel for the lower part of the hair is applied and fired once more. Finally, the details are added with white vitreous paint and the work is signed with liquid gold. Then, the piece is fired once more, for a shorter period of time, as is common for vitreous paints.

▼ **13.** View of the upper part of the hair when finished. The dry enamel shows differences in thickness that will produce the chiaroscuro effect typical of this technique.

Grisaille with Limoges White

Limoges white is made of sodium silicate and lead stearate, and is available as a very fine, almost imperceptible, ground powder. Combined with an oil essence, it is made into a paste following a process similar to that used for vitreous paints. Once a homogeneous paste is achieved, it is applied with a technique similar to painting. Distilled water, mixed with a few drops of very purified methylcellulose glue and left to rest for a minimum of 24 hours, can also be used as a binder. It is applied the same way as the other paste, but it has a quicker drying time, which makes it easier for working with sgraffito, as well as for applying glazes and gestural work; however, it cannot be used to create as many reliefs or reliefs with the same precision. It is white in color and semitransparent; if it is applied thinly, the color of the support over which it was applied can be seen. Grisaille with Limoges white is done by superimposing layers to create a chiaroscuro effect. However, it differs from the opal grisaille technique in that it does not produce such a wide range of tones. Its results have more contrast and a harsher luminosity, at least with the materials that are currently available. It cannot be used on very large surfaces when mixed with oil essence as a binder, and the evaporation and firing processes are more complex than with regular enamel. Evaporation is a critical and extremely important process. It should be slow, as with vitreous paints, or even slower. If it is not done properly, Limoges white can turn matte and

opaque, bubbles can form, and it can become brittle. Evaporation can be carried out in a pre-heated oven or with a laboratory alcohol lamp. Firing is just as important because Limoges white tends to shrink after each firing session, and it can vanish if it is fired too long. Next, Andreu Vilasís shows how a piece is made using Limoges white.

► **1.** The Limoges white is prepared on a sheet of dark glass (agate can also be used). A small amount of powder is dispensed with a palette knife, and a couple of drops of paraffin are added using a glass rod.

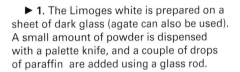

▲ **2.** Only the amount needed for each application is prepared; otherwise it can clump up and become unusable. A very small amount of oil is added because a little goes a long way. It is mixed with a palette knife to make a homogenous paste that does not run.

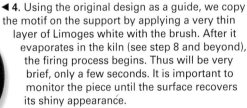

▲ **3.** Here, we use a copper support that has been covered with a layer of very dark cobalt blue enamel, applied directly, without flux.

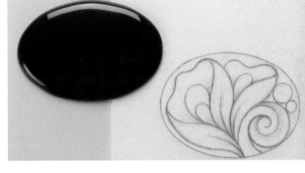

◄ **4.** Using the original design as a guide, we copy the motif on the support by applying a very thin layer of Limoges white with the brush. After it evaporates in the kiln (see step 8 and beyond), the firing process begins. Thus will be very brief, only a few seconds. It is important to monitor the piece until the surface recovers its shiny appearance.

◄ **5.** A second layer of Limoges white is applied with the brush, distributing the material with the metal tip to create the details. This layer should be thicker than the first one.

► **6.** The work continues in an orderly fashion. A thicker layer is applied in the areas that should look whiter (the petals in the foreground), and the rest of the elements are done with gradations. Finally, the circular designs are painted.

▲ **7.** The finished second layer before evaporation and firing.

▲ **8.** Evaporation is done in the kiln. The planche, previously heated to a working temperature of 1,650°F (900°C), is removed from the kiln and the piece is placed on it. It is inserted with tongs into the kiln, where it stays for a few seconds, and is then pulled out immediately.

▲ **9.** When taken out of the kiln, the piece will give off smoke and a characteristic odor produced by the burning oil. It is kept outside of the kiln twice the amount of time that it was inside and until it stops giving off smoke.

▲ **10.** In the first stages, the Limoges white turns dark brown and opaque. It gradually becomes grayish white as the paraffin oil evaporates.

◄ **11.** The process is repeated as many times as needed, until the Limoges white acquires its original color and a matte surface. It is kept outside the kiln one last time and then it is fired.

▲ **12.** View of the second layer after being fired.

◄ **13.** The last layer is applied. The final touches highlight the chiaroscuro and define a few areas. It is left to evaporate and fired one last time.

◄ **14.** The finished grisaille.

Colored Enamel: Dry Application

Dry application of enamel allows for quick progress, which is ideal for large-scale work and for working in multiples. The enamel is applied directly by sifting it through a mesh. The holes in the mesh should be somewhat larger than the size of the enamel particles. This method is very useful for working with stencils and for incorporating decorative elements in the piece. The processes used for cleaning the metal and removing the oxide have been explained and are the same as for the other techniques we have seen. A mask with a filter for dust and particles must be used. In this example, we show the process of making several different pieces that are part of a series created as a commission for company Christmas gifts. No counter coat is applied to the back since the layers on the front side will be very fine and not cover the entire surface. The copper support is 0.031 in (0.8 mm) thick, enough to resist warping. The enamel is applied dry, using stencils along with other techniques like applied enamel threads and vitreous paint for minor retouching. Thus, these pieces are examples of juxtaposed techniques, or mixed techniques, as it is commonly called. The appropriate metal thickness for making a piece similar to this one (4.75 × 4.75 in, or 12 × 12 cm), without a counter coat on the back, is between 0.025 and 0.04 in (0.7 to 1.0 mm).

▲ Montserrat Mainar (Barcelona, Spain). *Profiles*, 1990. Flux and opaque white enamel applied dry, details in matte black vitrifiable paint. 13.75 × 18.5 in (35 × 47 cm).

▲ **1.** Clean, degreased copper is used for the support. Two maple leaves, which have been pressed, are used as stencils. They are placed directly on the copper with the help of tweezers.

▲ **2.** Flux is applied with a sifter from about 4 in (10 cm) above the support, tapping it lightly to make the flux fall. The application is not even; it is only done around the edges of the stencils. The flux is applied just as it comes from the manufacturer, without washing it first.

▶ **3.** The leaves are very carefully removed with the tweezers to avoid disturbing the flux, since this would affect the outlines of the shapes.

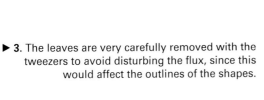

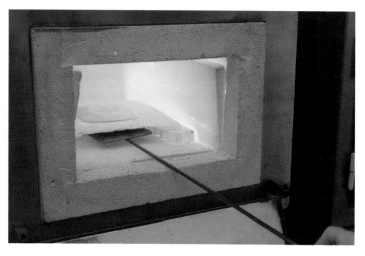

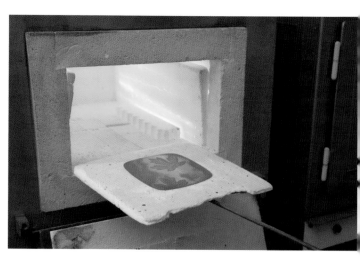

▲ **4.** The first firing is carried out. The kiln is turned on and heated to 1,650°F (900°C). The ceramic fiber planche is removed and the enamel piece is set on it using a spatula; then both are replaced in the kiln.

▲ **5.** The door is opened to control the firing and observe the behavior of the enamel. It must acquire a reddish tone, so the firing will be briefer than in other cases. The piece is removed when it begins to show a bright red color.

► **6.** The enamel is allowed to cool. It will cool faster than the metal, which is still ductile. This is the moment to eliminate any deformations by pressing the piece between two spatulas or irons. As it cools, a layer of cupric oxide (calamina) will appear on the copper that has not been covered with flux, and this will have to be removed with running water.

▲ **7.** This is the first layer of another piece. The half-fired flux has a red color caused by the effect of cupric oxide. Longer firing times will create results more like those shown in the previous illustration (step 6); it all depends on what the artist decides for each piece.

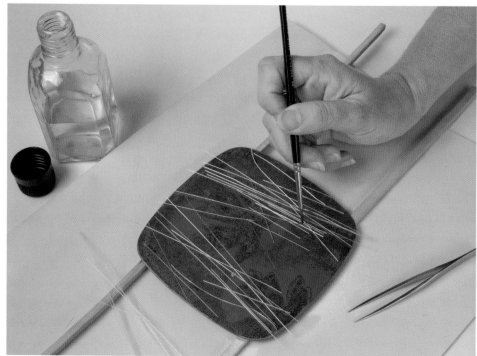

► **8.** The next phase consists of applying threads onto the flux layer. They are placed with tweezers where the artist desires and attached with a little tragacanth glue (or methylcellulose glue), which is applied at points along the thread with a brush.

▲ 9. The piece is fired again, staying in the kiln until the threads are bonded and shiny in appearance, and look like they are fused to the support. Then the calamina is removed.

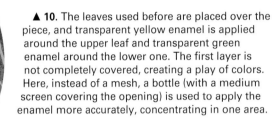

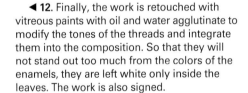

▲ 10. The leaves used before are placed over the piece, and transparent yellow enamel is applied around the upper leaf and transparent green enamel around the lower one. The first layer is not completely covered, creating a play of colors. Here, instead of a mesh, a bottle (with a medium screen covering the opening) is used to apply the enamel more accurately, concentrating in one area.

► 11. The piece is fired a third time, and afterward the oxide is removed. The result is a gradation of colors and shading.

◄ 12. Finally, the work is retouched with vitreous paints with oil and water agglutinate to modify the tones of the threads and integrate them into the composition. So that they will not stand out too much from the colors of the enamels, they are left white only inside the leaves. The work is also signed.

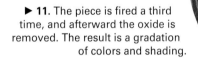

▲ 13. A finished piece from the series.

Painting on Enamel

Painting on enamel is considered a separate technique from enameling, although it is closely related to it. Its processes, application techniques, and results are nearer to painting than the rest of the enameling techniques. In fact, it is quite similar to painting on porcelain. However, there are also specific processes used in enameling that are fundamental to this technique, like the preparation of the support and the firing of the layers, among others.

Painting on enamel involves painting vitreous materials on a support that is first prepared with a fired layer of opaque white enamel. It has various applications, using either oil- or water-based materials, but miniatures are the most representative and important. Industrial enamels, screen-printing, and decals made of vitreous materials can also be used with this technique.

▲ Andreu Vilasís. Cap, 2007. Miniature, silver foil, vitreous paint, and silver. 1.5 × 1.5 in (4 × 4 cm).

Miniature with Oil Technique

Painting miniatures requires great technical control of various processes. Vitreous paints are mixed to create an oily paste that has the look and consistency of oil paint that can be applied with a brush. It is important to know the characteristics of the colors you will be using, both for making the mixtures and firing. Generally, if the colors are of good quality, and preferably from the same manufacturer, it is possible to mix the tones and colors that you need. (However, the warm color range—reds, oranges, and pinks—is usually more problematic.) It is also important to know how the paint will react to firing, and this is only possible if samples are made to establish the possible changes in color and the paint's general behavior in the kiln. The

◀ 1. First a full-size design is drawn for use as a guide for drawing on the support.

▶ 2. All miniatures require careful planning. The work should be carried out in a dust-free environment and protected with covers or glass domes. It is also a good idea to use the proper size support. Vitreous colors are prepared on a palette consisting of a piece of glass on a white base. They are applied with a special brush, which has a very fine, conical point, and short bristles designed for miniature work.

▲ 3. Each color is mixed separately. Paraffin is added, and the colors are kneaded with a spatula until a thick but fluid paste is created.

▲ 4. When choosing the colors that will be used, their behavior during firing and their final appearance must be considered. Samples and palettes that you have previously made are helpful for this purpose. As the different colors are prepared, they are placed on a glass sheet resting on a piece of white paper with a grid drawn on it, and references (number, name, or manufacturer) are noted on the paper.

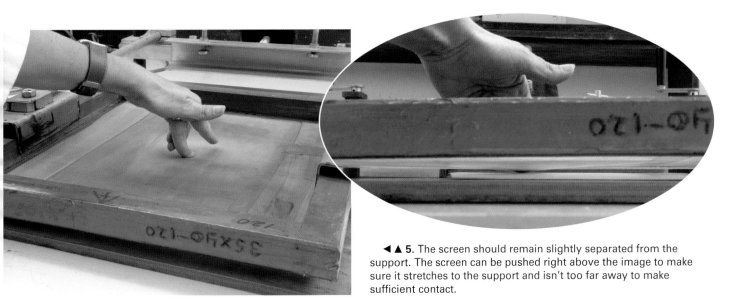

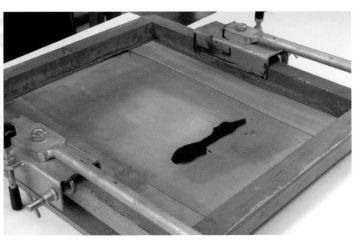

◀▲ **5.** The screen should remain slightly separated from the support. The screen can be pushed right above the image to make sure it stretches to the support and isn't too far away to make sufficient contact.

▲ **6.** A thick line of paste is applied to the screen just above or to the side of the image where the emulsion is hard (blocking the screen), using enough to make the impression.

▲ **7.** The paste is spread with the squeegee, which is held at a 45-degree angle. The squeegee should be slightly wider than the image and pulled across the screen quickly while applying even pressure. The screen and other tools should be cleaned with universal solvent, never alcohol, which will dissolve the emulsion.

▲ **8.** The image printed on the support. It is then evaporated and fired just like vitreous paints.

▶ Núria L. Ribalta. Several works from the series *Step By Step*, 1999–2008. Painted enamel and silk screen on steel. 6 × 8 in each (15 × 20 cm).

▲ Núria L. Ribalta. *Finift 2*, 1998. Pre-enameled industrial steel plate, enamel applied dry with stencils, decal, and applied threads. 11.8 × 9.5 in (30 × 24 cm). Shown with the original decal.

Transfers

Applying transfers (decals) cannot strictly be considered a technique, but it is one of many approaches used for creating enamel work. It is not a kind of painting either, but it is included in this section because its results are similar to painting. Furthermore, it is applied to the same kind of support: opaque white enamel on a perfectly smooth, homogenous, and level surface. In this example, with a support smaller than 10 in (25 cm) on each side, a sheet 0.02 to 0.024 in thick (0.5 to 0.6 mm) should be used. After the decal is applied, it is allowed to dry completely before firing. If there is any moisture, the water will boil during firing and create bubbles that can burst and break, deform, or crease the transfer. With the kiln set at normal working temperatures, the agglutinate is burned out to leave just the pigments. Finally the piece is fired, first with the door of the kiln partially open in case there are any traces of flammable materials. The piece is monitored until its surface is shiny, and then it is removed before it expands. Transfers are available in standard motifs, and it is also possible to order original designs. The transfers for enamelwork are the same as transfers used for decorating porcelain.

◀ **1.** The transfer, which will change to gold tones during firing, is applied to an industrial enameled steel support. The decal is shown here with its protective paper cover.

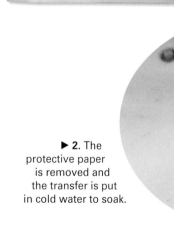

▶ **2.** The protective paper is removed and the transfer is put in cold water to soak.

▶ **3.** The decal is easily removed from the paper and applied to the support. It must be handled carefully to avoid tearing it or damaging the emulsion that holds the vitreous pigments.

▶ **4.** The image is situated correctly and smoothed with a soft, dampened sponge to remove bubbles and wrinkles as it is adhered to the support. A screen-printing squeegee can also be used, but this requires a certain amount of skill and much care.

▼ **5.** Here is the decal after transfer. It is allowed to dry 24 to 48 hours, depending on the humidity in the studio, in a dust-free environment.

▼ **6.** The kiln is turned on and brought to working temperature. The ceramic fiber or refractory planche is removed from the kiln and the piece is placed on it. This is done to avoid problems caused by thermal shock when the piece is placed in the kiln. The agglutinate is burned away by putting the piece in the kiln for only a moment, and then pulling it out right away. The burnout and evaporation should be done more slowly than for other vitreous paints because of the emulsion in the layer.

◀ **7.** The agglutinate or emulsion burns away, producing a lot of smoke. Flames should be avoided, although they frequently appear. This process is repeated as many times as needed until there is no more smoke. Then the piece is fired much like the harder enamels.

▶ **8.** The fired piece.

Champlevé

Champlevé is a technique based on creating cavities in a metal support following a design, and then filling them with enamel to make a surface with alternating areas of enamel and metal. Metal at least 0.04 or 0.08 in thick (1 or 2 mm) should be used for this technique. There are two methods of removing metal from the surface: cutting and extracting, or etching. The cutting is done with gravers, pushing the sharpened point into the metal to carve it away; metal burrs are raised as the support is cut away little by little. This technique requires much practice and skill, and it can be considered a specialty within the discipline of engraving. It is a good idea to have a professional engraver (see page 115) do it for you; we will not demonstrate it here as it is beyond the scope of this book. Etching is carried out in a bath of nitric acid or iron perchloride. The action of these products eats away the metal in areas that are not protected—that is, areas that are not covered by reserves. Reserves can be made with asphaltum, paraffin or wax, lacquer, or etching varnish (as in this example), as well as with plastic contact paper. Reserves are applied to the areas that you do not want to etch, and the sides and back of the metal must also be covered. Nitric acid etches the metal faster than iron perchloride, but when it contacts the metal it produces very noxious fumes, so you must be properly protected with gloves and a mask with a filter, and work in a place with an exhaust system. The metal is submerged in the bath face up and watched to note the depth of the etching and to eliminate the bubbles deposited on the metal (see page 68). With this method, the lines of the design are often slightly jagged because of the bite of the acid. Etching with iron perchloride (which we use here) is slower than using nitric acid, and although it does not produce as many fumes, it should be used in a well-ventilated place. The etching results are more perfect, with vertical walls and very sharp lines.

It is generally recommended that the depth of the etching be one half the thickness of the metal. When etching, at least 0.08 in (2 mm) of metal must be left around the perimeter, and separations at least 0.04 in (1 mm) between the excavated areas that will later be filled with enamel. When engraving, there are no limitations other than leaving a sufficient perimeter around the metal piece; the backgrounds can be engraved with line textures and other designs if transparent enamel will be used. Etching, however, allows you to create particular effects, etch different depths, and cover etched areas with new reserves and place the piece in another acid bath.

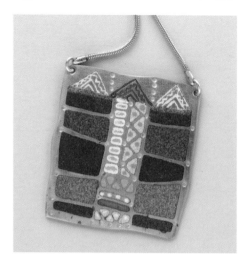

◀ Michèle Gilbert (Le Vigen, France). Pendant, 2002. Champlevé on copper and then silver plated. 1.97 × 1.77 in (5 × 4.5 cm).

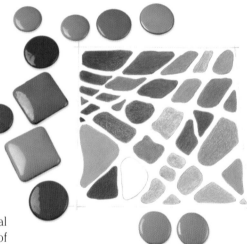

◀ **1.** The design is laid out at full size, leaving enough metal on the edges and between the enameled areas and balancing the enameled areas against the areas that are not enameled. Here we will use opaque enamels, but transparent enamels could be used as well. Opaque enamels can be applied in a thicker layer since they do not change over successive firings.

▶ **2.** Sheet copper 0.047 in thick (1.2 mm) will be used for this project. It is marked to the desired size and cut with a saw, as shears will only cut pieces 0.04 in (1.0 mm) and less.

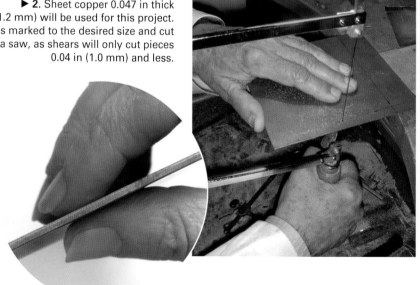

▶ **3.** This piece will be done without a counter coat. The counter coat can be omitted if the piece is thick enough (more than 0.04 in [1.0 mm]), if not very much metal has been carved away, and if it will only be fired a few times. Otherwise, a counter coat should be applied to keep the support from warping and the enamel from cracking.

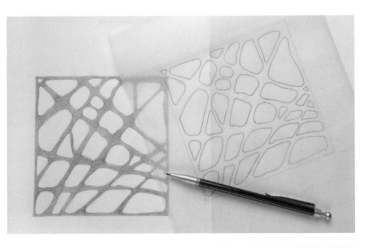

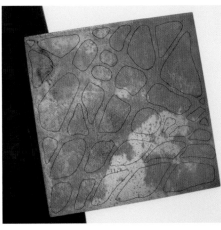

◀◀ **4.** The original design is traced, marking the areas of the reserves with a pencil—that is, the places where the metal will not be etched. Then the shapes are copied to a piece of tracing paper and applied to the support, which has been cleaned and degreased (see pages 68–69) with black carbon paper.

◀ **5.** The back of the piece is protected with a sheet of plastic contact paper that is a little larger than the metal for easier handling.

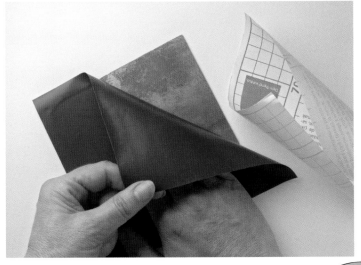

PROBLEM: EXCESSIVE ETCHING

You can control etching by looking at the piece every fifteen minutes or so—checking the condition of the reserves and the removal of the metal. Make sure to check carefully because excessive etching can cause holes in the piece.

◀▲ **6.** Using the original as a guide, the reserves are painted with varnish. The edges of the metal are protected first and then the zones on the face that are to be masked. The varnish is applied with precision, using a generous coat to cover the protected areas well, and then it is left to dry completely.

◀ **7.** Since the etching will be done with iron perchloride, the piece is placed in the bath with the reverse side up. Corks are applied with contact cement (without over-lapping protected areas) to keep the surface from coming into contact with the bottom of the tray, which would cause the etching to be uneven and have gaps.

◀ **8.** The piece is placed in the tray with a solution of 10 to 15% water and 85 to 90% pure iron perchloride. Gloves should be worn, and plastic or glass tools should always be used. The bottom is facing upward so that the metal particles will fall to the bottom of the tray, which will enhance the corrosive action of the perchloride. The piece is occasionally removed and observed to control the etching.

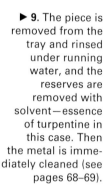

▶ **9.** The piece is removed from the tray and rinsed under running water, and the reserves are removed with solvent—essence of turpentine in this case. Then the metal is immediately cleaned (see pages 68–69).

▲ **10.** The enamels are applied with a spatula, pressing on them to completely fill the depressions. Nib pens or steel scribes can also be used to fill small, narrow spaces and corners. A generous amount is deposited, pushed to the edges of the depression, and left higher in the center in the shape of a drop. Then it is allowed to dry. Keep in mind that this is a slow process because of the thickness of the application.

▶ **11.** Firing requires more time than other techniques because of the thickness of the metal. The piece is removed when the enamel looks uniform and shiny. It is left to cool, and then the oxide (calamina) is cleaned off the copper. During firing, the enamel particles completely melt and run together, and the spaces that were between them disappear, reducing the thickness of the layer. Thus, it is necessary to add enamel, fire, and clean the piece a few times to fill the openings to the level of the metal.

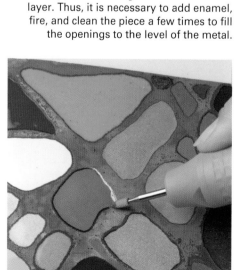

◀◀ **12.** The last firing is done and the oxide cleaned with water. The areas between the enamel are polished with a tungsten bit with a narrow tip to eliminate the black oxides mixed with enamel that form in the hollows where the enamel and metal meet. If the surface of the enamel is scratched lightly, it will become matte. To return its shine, it can be cleaned with fiberglass and ammonia and water, and then fired lightly. The calamina can be eliminated with salt and vinegar (see page 69).

► **13.** Finally, the surface of the metal is ground and polished with a rubber-tipped bit. This should be done very carefully, especially if the piece is going to be plated with gold, silver, chrome, or nickel. Any defects will become visible later, and they will be even more apparent after

the electroplating. Remember that the metal plate (gold in this case) will adhere to the metal support (copper) by conduction, and any trace of enamel or calamina will impede good adhesion.

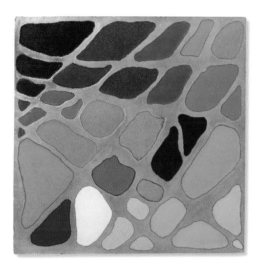

▲ **14.** The piece after polishing.

▲ **15.** The piece can be finished by having it electroplated with gold.

The hollow areas are etched into the metal. It is a small piece, 0.04 in (1 mm) thick. In this case, plasticene is used to make the supports for the plate.

The enamel is applied to each design, in some cases covering the reserved metal. Notice how the piece looks after the last firing.

The metal is stoned to remove excess enamel and make it level with the metal. A rough carborundum stick is used in the first phase, working wet and holding the stick flat against the surface of the work. Next, it is stoned with a finer carborundum stick, then with alundum, and finally with fine sandpaper.

The metal is polished with a rotary tool and a rubber or emerald bit to remove scratches from the surface. A last, very quick firing is done to return the sheen to the metal. Mechanical polishing can also be done using glass or pumice pastes or tripoli powder, or superfine sandpaper and an electric sander. Finally, the piece is silver plated.

This method is best for making small pieces, like jewelry, or larger pieces with small designs with narrow lines or spaces that are difficult to fill without flowing over the edges of the metal. This method results in works where the enamel and metal form a continuous surface.

Cloisonné

Cloisonné is a technique that involves enameling cells that are created by attaching metal wire to the support. The cells follow the shapes of the design, and they can be fixed to the support with a layer of enamel or soldered directly to the metal. The metal support must be from 0.01 to 0.028 in (0.3 to 0.7 mm) thick, according to the size of the piece, regardless of the technique being used. The support is fired in the kiln to attach the wires to the enamel layer. Or, if they are to be soldered directly to the metal, a torch is used to apply heat from the bottom of the piece. If the first method is used, the layer of flux or enamel should be hard and not too thin (see pages 60–61), so that the wires do not sink too far into the layer, causing the walls of the cells to be too low. If the work is done with silver wire, the firing should be done at a lower temperature than usual, around 1,560 to 1,580°F (850 to 860°C). It is important to control this process, because if the silver makes contact with the copper it will melt and become solder. This will cause dark or yellowish blotches and cause the wire to disappear from the surface of the piece, which isn't helpful. In this case, the working temperature affects the choice of enamels, which cannot be too hard. (This shows the importance of knowing the characteristics of enamel and of making samples

▲ David Chkheidze (Tbilisi, Republic of Georgia). Pendant, 2007. Cloisonné with silver on copper, silver setting with rhodonite cabochon. 2½ × 2 in (6.3 × 4.8 cm).

and palettes beforehand.) Also keep in mind that some of the warm range of colors will be altered when they come into contact with the silver (see page 26).

The cells are formed with the help of tweezers and pliers, using the original design as a guide, and the extra pieces are cut off. When designing the motif, the shapes of the cells must be studied carefully: It is a good idea not to break up the design into too many lines. A straight piece should be joined to another straight piece to form an angle; if not, they will lean over during firing. Lines can be curved or angled, but it is best to avoid making too many lines meet at one point. This can make it difficult to apply enamel in the interstices, and grime can collect there if the support isn't covered adequately. Of course, it is not possible to make the wires cross each other, and too many wires grouped together can cause tensions and cracks in the enamel. For these reasons it is advisable to make fairly basic shapes with the wires. The cells are filled by applying the enamel with a spatula or a brush. If you are using opaque enamels, it is possible to fill the cells completely, forming a drop in the middle as is done in the champlevé technique (see page 104); however, this should not be exaggerated because the center can ball up too far. When it comes to transparent enamels, it is preferable to apply them in several layers, firing the piece each time.

Keep in mind that, when applying several layers of enamel, the wire will lean toward the side where the enamel layer is thicker. When creating pieces with vertical walls, like pitchers or sculptures, the enamel is mixed with a few drops of special vegetable glue (from the *funori* algae, the purple orchid, or highly purified pumpkin seeds), which will

▶▶ **1.** First the design of the piece is created. In this case, it is the decoration for the lid of a jewelry box, combining two techniques: cloisonné for the central motif and basse-taille on the four side pieces. Notes on the colors for the design are also made and used as a guide during the creation of the piece.

▶ **2.** A copper support 0.03 in (0.8 mm) thick is used for the support. The central diamond is cut out with a saw; it will be used for the cloisonné, and the four corner pieces will be used for the basse-taille technique. They are marked to avoid confusion.

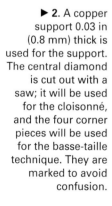

▶ **3.** The metal is cleaned. A counter coat of enamel is applied to the back and a layer of flux to the front, and then it is fired. Next, the designs are traced onto it.

strengthen the enamel until it is fired. When it comes to cleaning, the common steps used for all techniques can be followed. The greatest drawback of working with a copper support and wire is the oxide that is produced after each firing, which must be removed. If you are using copper wire, the regular cleaning method can be used (see pages 68–69) with vinegar, since acids can affect enamels, especially the opaque ones. If only the support is copper, the oxide is removed from the edges only. After the piece is finished, the relief of the wires and the enamel may be left (through capillary action, the thickest areas are where the enamel is in contact with the wires), or you can stone the piece to achieve a uniformly smooth finish. There are several ways to do the stoning, which will be explained later.

▶ **4.** In this exercise the cloisonné is made using silver wire 0.004 in thick and 0.047 in high (0.1 × 1.2 mm). Each cell is made using the design as a guide, shaping it with tweezers and pliers until it matches the design.

▲ **5.** The wire is cut directly from the roll to the exact size of the cell with wire cutters.

▶ **6.** The wire is situated on the support with tweezers so that it lines up with the traced shapes.

◀ **7.** Next, a drop of methylcellulose glue is carefully applied to fix the wire to the support and prevent it from moving during work. Glue can also be applied to the entire cell before it is placed, although this uses more glue and the result is not as clean.

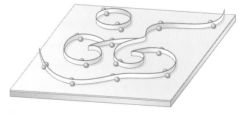

▶ **8.** Drops of enamel or special flux for silver on both sides of the wire can be substituted for the glue.

▼ **9.** Work continues on the motif with silver wire, and the glue is allowed to dry slowly. The piece is placed near a heat source (kiln) or under a strong light. Notice that the work has a profusion of straight lines on the sides. To keep them from leaning, the shapes of the cells are extended past the edge of the support, bent to form a U-shaped angle. This will hold them correctly, and several walls can thus be made with the same wire.

▼ **10.** The piece is fired to attach the silver wire to the flux. This will be faster than a normal firing, taking about one third the normal amount of time. To control the process, a small ball of enamel is placed on each side of a shape (a petal, for example) and is watched during firing until it shows a rough surface; then the piece is removed. If the wires are elevated, do not continue to fire. Just remove the piece and, while it is still hot, gently push them down with a wide spatula to correct the situation. Then let it cool.

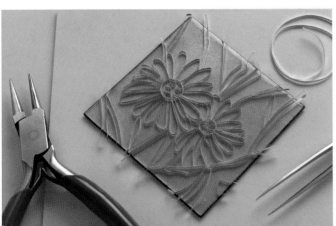

▲ **11.** The enamel is applied with a brush and, if necessary, packed with a steel point to fill all the cavities and corners.

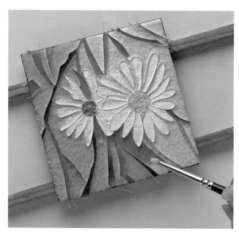

▲ **12.** We continue to fill the cells. In some we deposit a generous amount of opaque enamel that almost reaches the top of the cell, and in others we apply a thinner layer of transparent enamel.

LAYERS OF ENAMEL

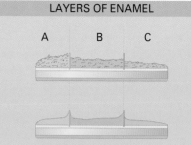

Filling the cells is done in phases, since during firing the thickness of the enamel is reduced. The enamels are applied wet; the opaque colors (A) can be applied in a thicker layer than the rest, almost to the top of the wire. Other colors (B) are applied in a normal layer about halfway up the wire, while transparent color gradations (C) can be created with several fine layers. After firing, the enamel is a bit higher where it touches the wire because of the capillary effect and the difference in thickness between the different enamels.

◀ **13.** The piece is fired for the first time.

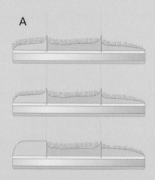

More layers are added and fired. The opaque enamels (A) reach the top of the wire in two or three phases because they can be applied in thick layers. We continue applying the rest of the enamels as described to fill the cells.

Most of the enamels (B) require three or four phases to reach the top of the wires.

▲ **14.** The counter enamel is touched up and a second layer is applied to level the enamel. The counter enamel is retouched again, and the piece is fired a second time.

▲ **15.** A third application is still needed to level the enamel. A blended opalescent color is also added to the background as well as a new color (at the top of the piece in the illustration), which will correspond to the shapes of the basse-taille corner pieces in the finished work. It is fired again and the overhanging wires are cut with pliers.

When very thin layers (C) are applied, four or more phases may be necessary to reach the desired height. If you do not wish to darken a color more, a final flux coat is applied to level the layers.

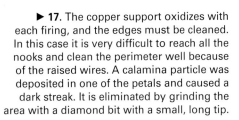

◄ 16. The oxide is removed from the edges of the support with a carborundum stick and the ends of the wires are smoothly rounded off.

► 17. The copper support oxidizes with each firing, and the edges must be cleaned. In this case it is very difficult to reach all the nooks and clean the perimeter well because of the raised wires. A calamina particle was deposited in one of the petals and caused a dark streak. It is eliminated by grinding the area with a diamond bit with a small, long tip.

◄◄ 18. A drop of white enamel is put on the scraped area. Transparent enamels of different colors are also applied to create a light gradation on the petals and some of the leaves. Finally, a second layer of yellow is added over the green shape in the background (right-hand corner of the photo) and another shape is made that will match up with the basse-taille corner pieces. A fourth firing is done.

▼ 19. To finish, a new layer of color is added to strengthen the gradation on the petals and on the center buttons of the flowers, and a new layer is applied on the two shapes in the background. Light blue opalescent enamel is also added to the background of the composition to make a slight mother-of-pearl gradation that can be seen on the sides of the upper part of the piece. Then it is fired for the last time.

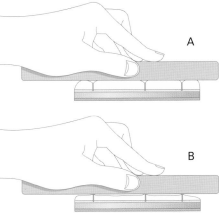

◄ 20. The relief of the wires and the smooth, shiny enamel was left on this piece. If a smooth surface is desired, it must be stoned. This is done in phases: You begin with a very rough stone, then switch to a finer one or a diamond pad, and continue with increasingly finer ones. The abrasion raises the surface of the enamel and makes a matte finish; this should always be done wet, preferably under running water. Making the enamel and metal smooth and even will be more or less laborious depending on how much higher the enamel is than the wire. For example, it will be more work in case A than in B. It is best to stop the enamel at the level of the wire or to apply flux. The piece is cleaned with fiberglass and ammonia to remove the particles. Finally, before proceeding to the final firing to return the glossy finish to the enamel, the piece is submerged in a container of distilled water brought nearly to a boil to eliminate the particles encrusted in the pores.

A

B

Smooth Satin Finish

A smooth satin finish is achieved by leveling the piece with stones in different phases and a final polishing of the surface of the piece, without a final firing. After the cloisonné work is done, a final coat of flux can be applied to level the surface of the work. It can be applied over the entire piece, but it is more common to put it only on the areas that need it to make a uniform surface. It can be done dry with a small sifter or with a spatula for more precision. Next it is fired and the surface is stoned wet, a multi-step process. First the surface is leveled using different carborundum sticks or diamond pads (very useful for curved pieces), and work progresses from rough to fine sticks, washing the piece well in tap water with each change of grit. The result is a rough, matte surface. Next comes polishing, which is also done in several steps, starting with light abrasives like pumice. Then the piece is scrubbed with special types of vegetable charcoal, always wet, which will give it a somewhat satiny finish. After this step, the piece is washed under running water and then with ammonia and a fiberglass polisher to remove any possible traces of charcoal left on the enamel; it is a good idea to do this cleaning ultrasonically or take it to a specialized studio. The semi-glossy marble-like texture is achieved by applying special products and burnishing the piece by hand to create a deep satin sheen. Pieces with this finish have a special feel. In the next example, we demonstrate

▶ Kioko Iio (Tokyo, Japan). *Composition*, 2007. Copper with repoussé and cloisonné. 15⅜ × 14⅛ × 11 in (39 × 36 × 28 cm).

the entire finishing process. The piece was made following a process similar to that of the previous example, but it was given a preliminary coat of opaque white enamel that acts as a sort of flux coat, causing the colors to have pastel tones. In this case, the colors were applied in the cells as gradations and flowed over the tops of the cells and into the others, where cylindrical silver inclusions were added.

▲ **1.** The cloisonné is created with successive applications of enamel and firings. The cylindrical silver inclusions are added before the second-to-last firing, placed at the artist's discretion with tweezers. It is fired, and then the last layer is applied and the piece is fired again.

▲ **2.** A final layer of flux is added with a small sifter over the low spots of the piece to make a more uniform surface, and it is immediately fired.

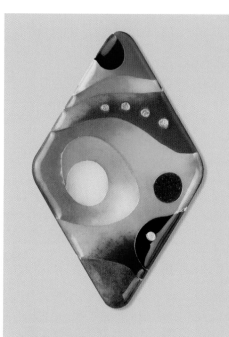

▲ **3.** The result is a smooth, glossy enamel piece.

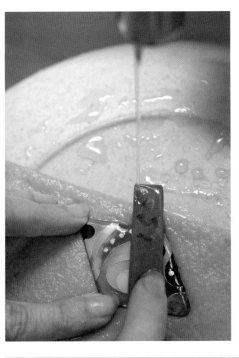

◄ **4.** Stoning is done with water, the surface rubbed evenly with a carborundum stick, without applying too much pressure. The work begins with a rough grit and finishes with the finest grit (from 150, moving on to 380, 400, 600, 800, and 1,000, approximately), washing the piece with running water after using each stick.

▼ **5.** Polishing is done manually, scrubbing with a pumice stone stick or powder, and then the piece is washed. Next, the surface of the enamelwork is scrubbed with charcoal made from magnolia (*Magnolia grandiflora*) and then with charcoal made from paulownia (*Paulownia tomentosa*), moving the charcoal in a direction perpendicular to its grain.

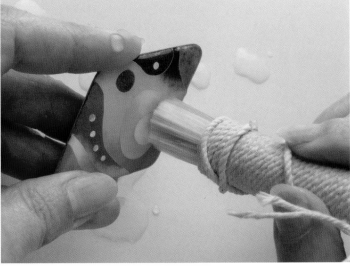

▲ **6.** The final cleaning is done with ammonia, scrubbing with fiberglass to remove possible particles and deposits in the surface of the enamel.

◄ **7.** The piece is dried and a finish is applied to make it shine. You can use beeswax dissolved in turpentine, furniture wax, or wax for marble or cars. When it dries, it is buffed with a very soft, clean cotton rag or a chamois to give it a deep, satiny shine.

Smooth Shiny Finish

Another possible finish involves leveling the piece with a final flux coat, stoning the surface with a carborundum stone, and polishing it with a polisher and very fine silica paper. This will create a very smooth surface, polished and shiny, with no need for a final firing. The sheen may be more or less intense, and even have a mirrored finish, depending on the level of polishing. This is the method employed in the creation of the work illustrated at the beginning of this section. All mechanical stoning processes, and those done with a rotary tool and bits, require the use of a dust mask and safety glasses.

◄ To make a glossy finish, an electric polisher with extra-fine waterproof papers is used. The papers used to polish the wet piece should get progressively finer, from 400 to 2,000.

Basse-taille

Basse-taille, also known as bas-relief, is based on making a subtle relief in the metal, which later will be covered with transparent enamel. This technique evolved from engraved champlevé and was sometimes used in combination with it, which sometimes creates confusion about the names. Basse-taille uses design motifs with very slight relief so that the background stands out around them. Or conversely, the design motifs are raised to create a three-dimensional effect. The relief can be created through different processes: by etching and with punches and burnishing tools, as well as by chiseling or cutting with gravers. In any case, working with these tools requires skill and practice. In addition, the artist must know and consider the peculiarities of the materials and apply them to the bas-relief technique. The enamel must be transparent, of course, and it is a good idea not to use colors that are too dark. They are applied somewhat dry with a brush or a spatula, with just enough moisture to spread them in an even, regular layer. This can also be done using dry enamels that have been washed so they do not lose transparency. The resulting layer should be even and smooth on the surface, despite the irregularities of the metal underneath. This will create the different intensities in color and light that this method is known for. In areas where the relief is deeper, there will be more enamel, with a deeper color but less light. In the areas where the metal stands out, there will be less enamel, which will have a lighter tone and be more luminous. The preparation and cleaning of the metal is done in the usual way, as is the application of the counter coat. Often, transparent enamel can be substituted for the counter enamel, to highlight the negative image on the metal created by the repoussé work or punches (see page 115). After application, the enamel is dried by evaporation (on a source of heat like the kiln or under a strong light), and then it is fired the usual way.

◄ Perote Armengol (Barcelona, Spain). *Liberty*, 1984. Painted enamel on acid-etched basse-taille. 6.3 × 6.3 in (16 × 16 cm).

Etched Bas-relief

The etched bas-relief process is similar to that of champlevé; it is done in a nitric acid bath. This acid rapidly etches the metal, but when it comes in contact with it very noxious fumes result, so gloves, a mask with a filter for fumes, and a well-ventilated place or studio with an exhaust hood are required. The piece is submerged in the tray facing up, so that the process can be carefully controlled and the bubbles that form on the surface of the metal removed. This method allows the creation of different levels of bas-relief by making successive reserves and acid baths. It is important to plan the work well and to control all of the steps. A wide range of products can be used for making the reserves (see pages 39 and 45).

In the next example, we demonstrate the creation of bas-relief with the corner pieces of the cloisonné enamelwork that was demonstrated in the previous section (see page 106). We will use copper sheets 0.032 in (0.8 mm) thick to create raised plant motifs in bas-relief.

► **1.** The shapes of the original design are traced on the four pieces, and they are redrawn with permanent marker. Then they are placed on the drawing so that the design lines up correctly. In this case, the designs are to be raised above the background, so they are reserved by painting lacquer on them with a brush, which will dry quickly. If you wish the designs to be reversed, the background of the composition should be covered with lacquer instead.

► **2.** It is a good idea to use colored lacquer for the reserves because it makes it easier to control the etching process. The four pieces are submerged faceup in the nitric acid bath, handling them with stainless steel or plastic tongs, and the etching process is observed carefully. It is very quick since only 0.028 in (0.7 mm) deep relief is required.

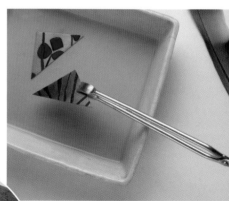

◄ **3.** The pieces are removed from the bath and the acid is neutralized by scrubbing the metal with a brush and bicarbonate with water. Next the lacquer is removed with alcohol. Finally, it is wet scrubbed with a stiff brush and fiberglass to remove all traces of acid and to polish it.

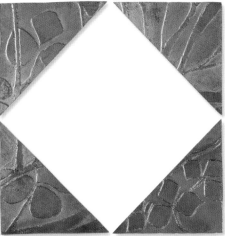

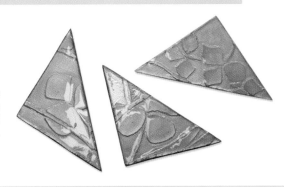

◀ **4.** The four pieces after making the bas-relief and being cleaned.

▶ **5.** Counter enamel is applied (see page 70) and a layer of flux, and then the pieces are fired. The oxide is removed from the edges after each firing.

▼ **6.** The pieces are placed in the kiln resting on supports that barely make contact with them, but are strong and stable. Here we use a steel support that holds the piece on three points.

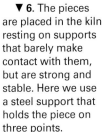

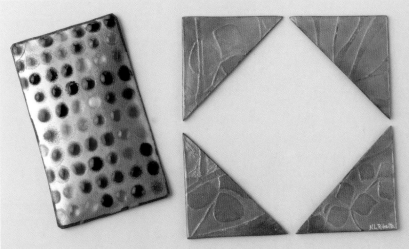

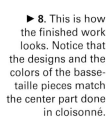

▲ **7.** Using a sample palette as a guide, a second layer of transparent enamels is applied following the color scheme of the original drawing, with a light gradation of colors.

▶ **8.** This is how the finished work looks. Notice that the designs and the colors of the basse-taille pieces match the center part done in cloisonné.

GUILLOCHE

Guilloche (from the French *guilloché*) is a term that describes certain ornamental patterns that are mechanically engraved by special machines. They are very intricate, repetitive motifs, with curved interwoven patterns that are slightly in relief. Nowadays they are mainly used in high-quality watch faces, especially in Switzerland. There are not many guilloche specialists, but today's technology has eased their task with magnification devices. Although guilloche is a mechanized decoration, it requires control in holding and rotating the piece. In this example, we see a round guilloche piece that has been enameled.

▲ **9.** The enamelwork decorates the top of a jewelry box.

Basse-taille with Burnishing Tools and Punches

Basse-taille can also be created with burnishing tools and punches. The former, besides being used for burnishing, can be used for making shallow relief in sheet metal by applying pressure and dragging the tool to create the lines of the designs. The width of the lines depends on the kind of tip and its curve. Designs can also be drawn using punches with spherical tips, which work very well for making dots.

In this method and that of engraving, the relief is negative—that is, working on one side of the sheet will cause the design to stand out on the other side. Traditionally, the enamel is applied to the side that is worked, which is considered the top, but nowadays it is possible to enamel the piece on either side, according to the particularities of each piece and the expressive intentions of the artist. The thickness of the metal used for this process ranges from 0.01 to 0.012 in (0.25 to 0.3 mm). In the next example, we demonstrate the creation of a piece in 0.012-in (0.3 mm) sheet copper, which is enameled on the side of the relief.

▲ 1. The piece is placed on a soft but resistant support and worked on one side to make a shallow groove. Using burnishing tools with fine, round tips, it is possible to make lines of different widths and dots.

◀ 2. Counter enamel is applied to the back of the piece, which in this case will be the working side, and a layer of transparent yellow enamel (which must be very clean) on the front, which will be the side that shows the relief. Notice the tonal gradations of the enamel and the luminous effect of the relief.

Punching

Punching consists of modeling the metal without cutting it or raising a burr. This results in one side of the metal with raised relief and the other side with negative relief. The work is done with punches to create shallow grooves that delineate the motif. The punch is held perfectly vertical, and the top end is repeatedly struck with a hammer to create the groove in the metal. The blows should be crisp and accurate, striking just once and then advancing the line slowly but surely without raising the punch from the groove; the process is repeated until the design is complete. When the forming is done, it may be necessary to work on the other side of the piece to finish some of the details. A good thickness for the metal is 0.02 in (0.5 mm); if greater relief is required, 0.24-in (0.6 mm) sheet metal can be used. Here we demonstrate the difference between the top, with incised grooves, and the back, with the motif in raised relief, both of them enameled.

▶ 1. The bas-relief is created with a punch on the front of the sheet metal, which rests on a soft but resistant surface. The metal piece is held in place with steel brads; for delicate work, a support similar to that shown in the next section on engraving is used. The punch is held vertically and struck with a single hammer blow.

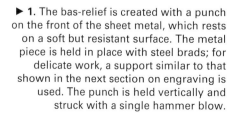

◀ **2.** This makes grooves that delineate the motif in shallow bas-relief. The back of the piece (in the image) shows the raised relief.

▲ **3.** The front is enameled with transparent dark blue. The grooves show a deeper color while the background shows a somewhat more luminous tone.

◀ **4.** The back of the piece. The raised lines create a different effect than those on the front.

Engraving or Cutting

Engraving is a traditional way of creating basse-taille works. It consists of removing metal with chisels or gravers. These tools require a certain amount of skill and practice to master the technique. The engraving is done with a graver, making cuts with the pointed tip, which should always be well sharpened, and pressure is applied as it is moved forward. The graver raises small burrs and the work progresses little by little. The metal piece is placed on a prepared support, consisting of a slab covered with soft mastic or tar, and is pushed into it, leaving the face exposed. When it has cooled and it is possible to comfortably work on the piece, it can be rotated and tipped while holding the slab with the other hand safely away from the graver. When the work is finished, the material on the support is again heated with a torch so that the piece can be removed easily and cleaned. The thickness of a sheet used for engraved basse-taille work should be between 0.4 and 0.8 in (0.1 and 0.2 mm). The best metals for this are copper and silver, the latter being more ductile and easier to work.

◀ Sarah Letts (Great Britain). Earrings, 2000. Basse-taille and mixed techniques. ½ × ⅜ in (1.4 × 1 cm).

▶ The metal piece is inserted and firmly held in the tar on the support. It is engraved with the tip of the graver, always pushing from back to front and keeping the hand that holds the support behind the one holding the tool, to prevent accidents.

Plique-à-jour

Plique-à-jour is also referred to as window enamel, because it simulates the techniques of architectural stained glass windows, which are made with leaded glass with enamel spread between narrow walls, like little windows. It is related to cloisonné, but it differs in that the enamel has no support or backing but is instead suspended in air. Thus, the proper enamel for this technique is transparent, but it is possible to use opalescent enamels to create certain effects. This technique requires complicated and somewhat difficult processes, and the application of the enamel is the most difficult of all. Very fine, wet enamels, mixed with distilled water as an agglutinate to a pasty texture, are the best for pieces that are not flat (see page 64). The enamel will adhere to the sides of the cells (or walls) through capillary action because of the surface tension of the water. After the piece is fired, the enamel is bonded strongly to the metal sides, forming a self-sustaining wall. Glue can be used on the sides of the openings to help the enamel adhere, and

► Gemma Moles (Barcelona, Spain). *Nu*, 2007. Plique-à-jour and vitreous paint on copper. 10 × 2⅜ in (25 × 6 cm).

◄ **1.** A pendant has been made from PHC metallic clay, silver in this case. The piece was constructed using a syringe applicator over a form made from a special clay (from the same manufacturer) that is modeled wet. Then the piece was fired and, as the clay baked, the support disappeared. Here, the thickness of the metal is 0.047 in (1.2 mm).

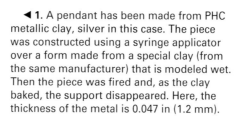

◄ **2.** The piece is carefully cleaned, and then enamel pastes are applied. These very fine enamels weigh less than others and are more homogenous when fired. With a brush, a small amount is deposited on the sides of the openings, more and more is added until the openings are full. As the enamels are applied, they are dried little by little with a clean rag or blotter paper to keep them from flowing off the walls with the water.

◄ **3.** The work begins at the highest areas of the piece because the enamel tends to move, drooping in vertical parts; the danger of it falling off increases the longer it takes to dry and be fired. In openings larger than about 0.2 in (5 mm), the entire opening should not be covered since the enamel can sag and fall off; only the sides should be covered.

◄ **4.** The piece is placed on a planche and the water is evaporated by passing it in and out of the kiln with the door open. During this task the temperature in the kiln will drop to about 1,475°F (800°C). When the enamel is completely dry, it is fired until it looks like an orange peel. In the first phases, it is best to leave the enamel a little underfired.

a few drops can also be mixed in so the enamel will be more solid when it dries. This must be a very pure and refined glue or it will affect the transparency. This technique is mainly used in jewelry work, and gold is the most commonly used metal. Silver is also used, but it has some drawbacks: its fusion temperature, which is near that of the enamels, and its color changes when used with enamels in the warm color range. Medium-hard or soft enamels should be used, and it is preferable for them to have the same fusion temperature (see page 60).

There are two ways to create the plique-à-jour: using temporary false supports made of gold or silver foil, or mica, or without using supports. In no case should the thickness of the metal used be less than 0.04 in (1 mm). However, artistic pieces are often made of thicker metal, in copper and silver. The holes can be cut in the metal with a saw, making the openings conical to help the enamel stay in place, although often pieces are made with lost-wax castings. It is possible to cover large openings with enamel on flat pieces (see the step-by-step pendant project on pages 144–145), but, small windows, not very narrow or long, are recommended to avoid the appearance of tension cracks. Before applying the enamel, it is very important to clean the piece by annealing it and washing it with detergent, because grease repels water (the agglutinate of the enamel) and makes the work impossible. Plique-à-jour requires very careful and somewhat tedious work, and it can be necessary to make a great number of applications and firings to finish a piece. Patience is also necessary, as you may not get the best results in the beginning. In addition, the piece must be handled very carefully at all times.

Here we demonstrate the process of creating a plique-à-jour piece, an original pendant by Gemma Moles.

▲ **5.** The piece is removed from the kiln and left to cool. Some of the larger windows are partially open, with the enamel on one side, and the enamel in the large hole in the center has mostly come loose and is hanging.

▲ **6.** The partial openings in the centers of the windows are filled, but at no time is enamel applied to an entire window over existing fired enamel. The enamel pieces that are hanging are removed completely.

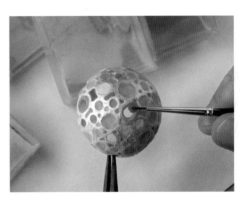

▲ **7.** Next, new enamel is applied to the inside edges of the window, and the old enamel is placed on it as if it were a cover. In some cases, it may be necessary to fire the piece in a position that favors the adhesion of the enamel to the edges of the window, or even to remove it completely and start over again. Generally, when working with different enamels, it is better to leave some of them underfired rather than firing others too much.

MICA SUPPORT

Before being used for the first time, mica is fired to remove any traces of moisture and organic material. Then it is exfoliated, separating the layers, to produce more pieces to use over a period of time. (See it used as a support for plique-à-jour in the step-by-step pendant project on pages 144–145).

▶ **8.** The process continues until all the windows are filled, and then a final firing is done.

▶ **9.** The piece is immediately put in a hydrofluoric acid bath to clean it and remove possible drops of enamel on the metal; this also smoothes the enamel and improves its transparency by eliminating a little of the surface layer. This must be done under a hood with an exhaust fan, while wearing gloves and protective gear. The piece is removed from the bath, and the action of the acid is neutralized by washing it with water and bicarbonate.

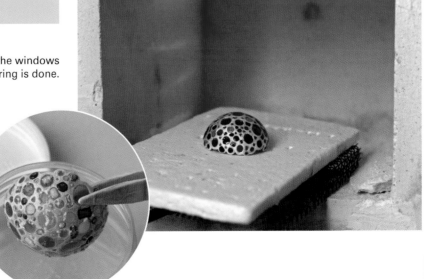

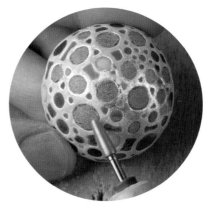

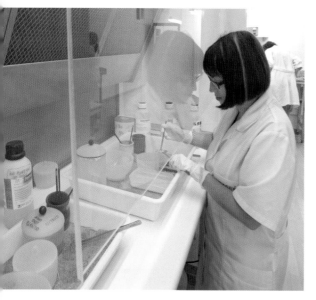

▲ **10.** In professional enameling studios, hydrofluoric acid is handled following very strict safety guidelines and under a ventilating hood specially designed for acids. If you do not wish to use acid, or cannot, the excess enamel can be removed using a rotary tool and a diamond bit.

▲ **11.** A rotary tool with a diamond-tip bit is used to remove traces of the enamel that the acid did not get. The surface of the enamel is opaque because of its contact with the acid and the rotary tool. It is scrupulously cleaned with ammonia and fiberglass, and fired a last time to return its shiny finish. If the metal is scratched it can be buffed with a rubber-tip bit, taking care not to encrust pieces of metal in the enamel, or it can be cleaned later in a hot bath.

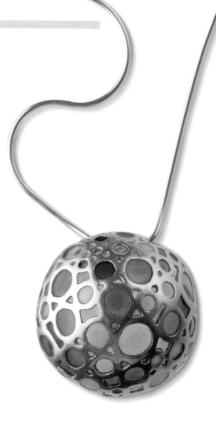

▲ **12.** Here is the finished pendant.

Plique-à-Jour on Large Pieces

The plique-à-jour technique can also be used to create large pieces with truly spectacular results. Here Montserrat Aguasca, an enameling student, demonstrates the creation of a bowl. Using a method similar to cloisonné, a grid or screen is made with silver wire on a temporary spun copper support, which will be removed after the enamels are applied and fired.

▲ ▲ **1.** First, a counter enamel is applied dry (by sifting) to the inside of the copper bowl (temporary support). Then flux is applied to the outside of the piece, and it is fired for the first time. Next, silver wires are attached following the technique described in the section on cloisonné. Since the piece has vertical walls, the wires are bonded with a special acrylic adhesive for vertical cloisonné. It is set aside to dry.

◄ **2.** The piece is fired to bond the wire to the flux, a quicker firing than usual. It is removed from the kiln, and if some of the wires are raised they are gently pressed down with a spatula while the piece is still hot. Then it is allowed to cool.

► **3.** The application of the enamel begins on the side of the piece, in the most vertical part of the bowl, and then it is fired.

◀ **4.** Work continues on the rest of the bowl and it is fired again.

▼ **5.** After the piece is finished, the temporary support is removed. A layer of black etching varnish is applied on the outside and on the top edge of the plique-à-jour piece to protect it from splashes and drips. It is left to dry.

▶ **6.** The counter enamel is removed from the inside of the copper bowl. To do this, a mixture of 30 percent distilled water and 70 percent hydrofluoric acid is put into the bowl. The acid is always added to the water, never the other way around. Protective gear should be worn and the work done under a ventilated exhaust hood. Notice how the acid reacts with the enamel.

▶ **7.** Once the traces of the counter enamel are cleaned out, it is neutralized with bicarbonate, and the copper bowl is then corroded away. This is done by putting one part distilled water and one part nitric acid in the bowl and allowing it to work while watching it carefully. The nitric acid in the water produces an exothermic reaction—that is, it creates heat. This can cause the varnish to come off in places, and the acid mixture may even boil and splash outside of the piece. It may be necessary to touch up the varnish. If it becomes too hot, the concentration of acid can be lowered by adding water.

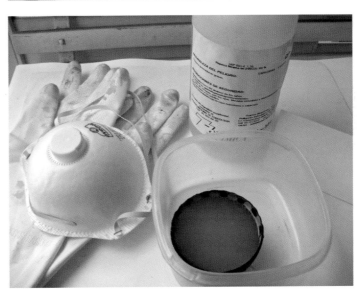

◀ **8.** The acid creates an oxidation-reduction reaction with the copper. Since this is a spun bowl with slightly unequal thickness in the walls, it is possible that the corrosive effect will not be completely uniform. The copper that is left can be eliminated by applying acid with a dropper or a brush.

▶ **9.** Finally, the varnish on the outside is dissolved with thinner or essence of turpentine. Here is the finished bowl.

Enamel in Relief

Enameling on relief or three-dimensional pieces (ronde bosse) presents us with a few challenges when it comes to the application and adhesion of enamels. After the metal has been formed to the artist's wishes and cleaned, it is time to apply the enamel. On medium and large pieces, it is best to apply it dry with a sifter. This is done in the same way as in the previous sections, by applying a coat of methylcellulose glue to the surface that is to be enameled and then depositing the enamel directly over it from the sifter. The sifter is held about 4 in (10 cm) above the work and tapped lightly to make the enamel fall on the piece, which is then sprayed with water to activate the glue. If necessary it can be retouched with a brush. The enamel can also be applied wet; very fine enamels are recommended for this, sifted until only micro-fine particles are left. Because they weigh less, they are less likely to slide off the surface of the metal. In all cases the enamel should be applied in very fine layers, and the amount of water must be controlled so that it does not wash the enamel from the metal. This is especially important when dry sifting on pieces with vertical walls, because if the layer is too thick and heavy it can move or fall off the piece (see the step-by-step "Centerpiece and Dessert Stand" project on pages 126–131). Adding very pure, refined glue to the enamel will help it adhere to the piece, although this may affect the transparency. Firing is a critical process, and often it will be necessary to use special supports to hold the piece. These can be made in the studio as they are needed; they should be stable and secure, and made so that the enamelwork makes contact with the support in as few places as possible so it will not adhere. These supports are especially important in the creation of work that will be enameled on all sides (see the previous example on page 127).

On some three-dimensional work with rounded surfaces, small pieces may flake a few days after firing due to contraction of the metal. An application of counter enamel is recommended, if possible, to help avoid this, and applying the enamel in thin layers is also helpful. The work must also be planned well, and as many tests as necessary should be done beforehand. It will be impossible to apply counter enamel to certain pieces—for example, on jewelry where transparent enamel matching the color of the work is used. Enamel adheres better to surfaces with relief (like a sculpture with folds of clothing) and texture, and sometimes small incisions can be made on the metal with a graver to help the enamel adhere better. Although most of these works are hollow, it is also possible to successfully enamel solid pieces of small size.

▲ Maria Berreklouw (Amsterdam, The Netherlands). *Frog*, 2007. Pendant of Colombian design, enamel in relief on cast silver. 0.47 × 1 × 0.6 in (1.2 × 2.5 × 1.5 cm).

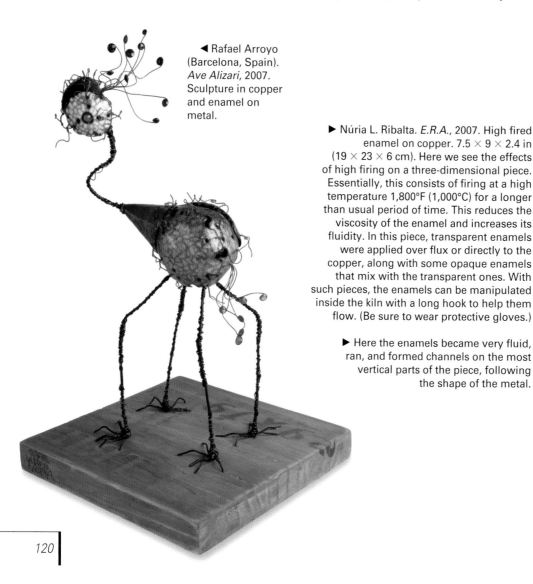

◄ Rafael Arroyo (Barcelona, Spain). *Ave Alizari*, 2007. Sculpture in copper and enamel on metal.

► Núria L. Ribalta. *E.R.A.*, 2007. High fired enamel on copper. 7.5 × 9 × 2.4 in (19 × 23 × 6 cm). Here we see the effects of high firing on a three-dimensional piece. Essentially, this consists of firing at a high temperature 1,800°F (1,000°C) for a longer than usual period of time. This reduces the viscosity of the enamel and increases its fluidity. In this piece, transparent enamels were applied over flux or directly to the copper, along with some opaque enamels that mix with the transparent ones. With such pieces, the enamels can be manipulated inside the kiln with a long hook to help them flow. (Be sure to wear protective gloves.)

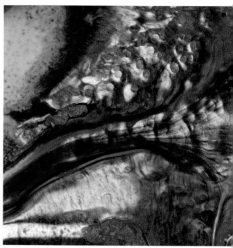

► Here the enamels became very fluid, ran, and formed channels on the most vertical parts of the piece, following the shape of the metal.

◄ **1.** Very fine enamels, almost in the consistency of a paste, can be applied wet. The enamel is applied systematically, a little bit at a time, to create a thin, uniform layer.

▼ **2.** The relief piece before cleaning; after cleaning, ready for enameling; and finished with transparent enamel.

Spheres and Beads

Enameling spheres and beads requires skill and practice to keep the enamel from running and coming off. The enamel can be applied dry or wet; in the latter case, a few drops of glue should be added to the enamel to improve its bond to the support. It is very important to keep the enamel from running, so excess water must be absorbed with a clean cotton rag. The spheres are held and manipulated with special jeweler's tweezers, and the piece is rotated as the enamel is being applied (firing supports can also be used for this).

If the metal is thick enough, and the piece won't be fired a lot, counter enamel is not needed, but it should be used in most cases to prevent deformation of the support. The counter enamel should be very fine enamel in slip (or barbotine); it is very fluid and often includes adhesive, depending on the manufacturer. It can be applied in a bath by submerging the sphere or bead in the slip and then removing it and turning it to evenly spread the counter enamel. Or, a syringe can be used to inject the counter enamel in the holes, turning it to spread it evenly.

▶ Berta Belza (Barcelona, Spain). Pendant and earrings, 2008. Painted enamel and silver foil on copper, mounted on a transparent glass ball with pieces of enamel and water. Pendant: 1 in (2.5 cm) diameter; earrings: ⅝ in (1.5 cm) diameter.

▼ Tweezers are used to hold and manipulate the spheres; here, however, curved pliers and a screw are used. The enamel is applied systematically and the water is occasionally absorbed with a clean rag.

▶ A firing stand made of a stainless steel rod and screen can also be used, which will help prevent oxides from forming during firing and cooling. The bottom of the screen is covered with paper or mica (if it is going into the kiln) to catch drops of enamel that would adhere to it during firing. During repeated firings, the position of the ball must be changed to keep the enamel from sagging as it becomes more fluid from the heat of the kiln. Afterward it is usually necessary to even out the thickness with a rotary tool or polisher with a carborundum bit.

Enameled Jewelry and Finishes

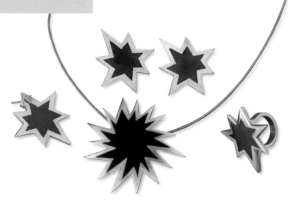

▲ Christina Weskott (Cologne, Germany). Himmelssterue, set with pendant, ring, and earrings, 1999. Enamel and gold-plated silver. Pendant: 2 × 1¾ in (5 × 4.5 cm); earrings and ring: 1⅜ × 1¼ in (3.5 × 3.3 cm) each. The red enameled earring is reversible.

The process of enameling gold and jewelry pieces is not essentially different from other enameling work, but there are some specific issues because of the materials and the pieces themselves. Thus, goldwork and jewelry are considered a specialization within the art of enameling. Gold and silver are the most commonly used metals, although the latter requires more care when it comes to preparation and the firing process, as its fusion temperature is near the working temperatures of enamels. Both gold and silver pieces should first be prepared and cleaned, including a good degreasing, before starting the enameling work. Applying the enamel requires some skill because the pieces tend to be small in size, and therefore difficult to handle, and they often have small details and tight areas. It is important to evaporate them well before moving on to firing, which is a very delicate process. The piece is placed in the kiln on a well-fitting, stable stand, supported in such a way that the enamel will not be damaged during firing. In most cases, stands will have to be made in the studio. In addition, some of the work may require help from a jeweler to assemble. Jewelry with mounted stones will require the help of a stone setter after the enameling is done.

When it comes to finishes, methods for working directly on the enamel will be shown in this section as well.

Protecting the Parts

Before enameling gold and other jewelry, it is of utmost importance to protect the soldered joints, rings, posts, wires, and other small elements and weak areas where enamel will not be applied. This will keep the parts from softening from the heat of the kiln and becoming deformed, and the solder from being destroyed. Thermal insulating paste can be used, and applied after each firing, or a paste made by mixing kaolin or refractory clay with distilled water, which must be dried completely before beginning to apply enamel. If you are using refractory clay, it does not have to be reapplied.

▲ Soldered joints and pins must be protected before beginning the enameling work. Here we use refractory clay mixed with distilled water to form a thick paste that is applied with a brush. Then it will be left to dry.

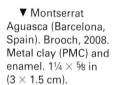

▼ Montserrat Aguasca (Barcelona, Spain). Brooch, 2008. Metal clay (PMC) and enamel. 1¼ × ⅝ in (3 × 1.5 cm).

Sliver and Metal Clay

Silver is a metal that requires great care during the firing process. Generally the working temperature in the kiln when firing enameled silver is about 1,500°F (820°C) to avoid problems. Sterling silver, used in jewelry work, has copper in the alloy, so it oxidizes each time it is fired; it is important to take the time to clean it to remove the oxide. Most enamels in the warm range (yellows, oranges, and reds) change when they come in direct contact with silver, so they must be isolated with a coat of silver flux to prevent changes in color and appearance. Some manufacturers sell special colors that can be applied directly to silver.

Metal clay (or PMC Art Clay brand) can also be used as a support for enameling. This product is easy to work with and very versatile, and pieces can be created in the studio rather than being commissioned from outside sources. In addition, it works very well for later enameling because it is fine silver (after firing it is 99% silver), not sterling silver, and there are no problems associated with oxides. It is handled just like clay, and a wide array of shapes and textures are possible. It is very useful for creating originals that can later be replicated as castings, and for making grid structures for the plique-à-jour technique. Since they have no soldered joints, they do

▲ The process of enameling a piece in the studios of Bagués-Masriera Jewelers, in Barcelona. This gold object is being enameled using the plique-à-jour and ronde bosse (relief) techniques, before the first firing. Notice the openings where precious stones will later be mounted. Work is done in phases, first the enameling and later the mounting.

not require any special preparation or protection. Natural elements (leaves, for example) or textiles can also be used as a sort of mold, by being covered with the clay. Firing is carried out according to the manufacturer's instructions, depending on the kind of clay, placing the piece on a refractory support or a ceramic fiber planche, and in the case of curved pieces, on a bed of vermiculite, a mineral from the mica group formed by aluminum, magnesium, and iron silicates. After firing it can be enameled, soldered, fired, drilled, and so on. It is possible to fire it several times as long as it is never above 1,650°F (900°C). PMC3 is one of the newest clays, and the best one for enamelwork. It has finer particles than the other clays, and it fires faster, resulting in a less porous and more compact structure; however, its firing temperature is lower than that of other clays. Pores result from the burning away of the organic agglutinate contained in the clay, and it is very important to eliminate any pores before applying enamel. It should be scrubbed using a brush with steel or fiberglass bristles, then degreased and cleaned. The enamels are applied and fired at 1,580°F (860°C). Tests should be carried out beforehand.

Finishes

Before beginning to polish or apply any finish (gold, silver, nickel, etc.), it is important to remove any traces of splashed enamel with a rotary tool and a diamond bit. An ultrasonic cleaning apparatus can be used for final polishing because it does not affect the enamel.

The surface of the fired enamel can also be given a matte finish without the use of abrasives. This is done by directly applying acid cream or acid salts that have been mixed with distilled water to make a creamy paste; this will cause a chemical reaction on the surface of the enamel that gives it a matte look. A brush or a wood spatula (never metal or glass) is used to apply them. Reserves can

be made to create a design, and a pattern can even be applied to the entire surface. This work must take place in a well-ventilated area, and the artist should wear gloves, safety glasses, and a respirator.

There are two ways of working with jewelry. Enamelwork can be made by the artist on a piece of copper and later taken to a jeweler, who will create a bezel, a base for a ring or a pin (see the jewelry on page 154). Or the artist can enamel directly on a support that was previously made by forming or spinning (see page 157).

Here are the details of the creation of two original hair clips by Núria L. Ribalta.

▶ **1.** Acid salts are applied directly to the fired enamel with a brush. In this case, reserves were made with blue adhesive plastic. The paste is allowed to work for 20 minutes and rinsed off with water; then the piece is neutralized with bicarbonate and cleaned.

◀ Christine Weskott (Cologne, Germany). *Wellen-Ring*, ring, 2000. Silver and opaque matte polished enamel. 1 × 1 × 1¼ in (2.5 × 2.5 × 3 cm).

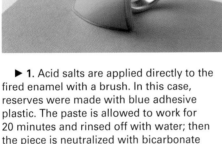

◀ **2.** The reserves are taken off. The enamel protected by the adhesive plastic looks shiny, while the rest of it is matte. The design can be seen in the contrast between the glossy and matte areas.

▲ Here we see the third application of ronde bosse enameling on a repoussé gold pendant figure, with the wings of the nymph already fired. The area that is to be enameled is cleaned with a cotton swab moistened with acid to remove the black copper oxide from previous firings, which is visible in the photograph on the areas that are not being enameled. After enameling is finished, the gems and pearls are set and the gold is polished to its original color. (Workshop of Bagués-Masriera Jewelers, Barcelona).

◀ Removing traces of enamel and polishing cast silver earrings by the Barcelona company Arior. Notice that the piece still has extra metal on the left from the casting process, which will be removed with a saw at the end of this step. Now it is used to help hold and manipulate the piece.

*I*n this chapter we demonstrate how a series of pieces were created and explain the process step-by-step. These five original projects were developed by different artists to show the complete working process, from the initial design to the finished piece. In all of them, the artists have used combinations of diverse techniques to create pieces that clearly reflect their particular styles, skills, and experience, and that serve as examples of the great versatility of this artistic discipline. Each step-by-step lesson offers a clear explanation of the formal and technical approaches the artist has employed. They are not meant to be used as examples for copying, but as a guide for developing your own working process—to help you find techniques that inspire you to create your own works of art.

Step by
Step

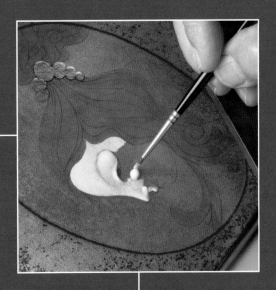

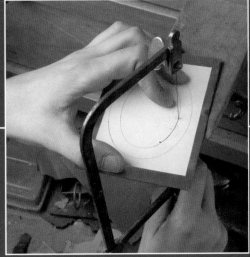

Centerpiece and Dessert Stand

*I*n this first step-by-step, we demonstrate the creation of a table centerpiece and a dessert stand or candy dish, by Núria López-Ribalta. Dry enamels are used for this work, in addition to the sgraffito technique, the application of gold and silver foils, and wet enamels to add color in certain areas. The artist has mastered the materials and has total control over the enamels and expressive qualities of gradation and sgraffito. Many approaches for the application and working of foils are wisely used in these two works of undeniable beauty and elegance. Understanding the behavior of copper during firing allows for the creation of gradations and textures, and the placement of the foils, worked with wrinkles and folds, masterfully configures textures and rhythms. The set is finished with silverwork on the feet and around the perimeter of the dessert plate.

▼ **1.** Three manufactured pieces of spun copper are used for this set, 0.032 in (0.8 mm) thick. The table centerpiece bowl (on the right) measures 7⅞ in (20 cm) in diameter, the foot of the dessert stand is a cylinder 2 in (5 cm) high, and the dish is 6¼ in (16 cm) in diameter (pieces on the left).

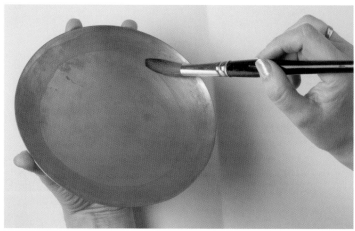

▲ **2.** Work begins with the dish of the dessert stand. It is annealed and thoroughly cleaned in a nitric acid bath to ensure that the enamel will adhere perfectly to the support. Next, highly refined tragacanth gum is applied to the back of the plate to completely cover it and on the top only around the edges. Special care is taken, only holding the edges, and the copper is touched as little as possible.

◄ **3.** Transparent enamels will be applied directly to the copper; they were cleaned by sifting just once, to remove the smallest particles, or the fines. Some tests were done previously to understand their behavior on the copper and with each other. During the processes of handling and applying the enamels, it is very important to wear a dust mask.

► **4.** The piece is set on the worktable, on two sticks and a sheet of paper, with the bottom facing up, and a thin, even layer of cobalt-colored enamel is applied to one side of the dish. The sifter is held about 4 in (10 cm) above the piece and tapped lightly.

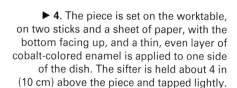

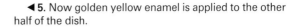
◄ 5. Now golden yellow enamel is applied to the other half of the dish.

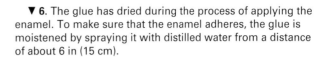
▼ 6. The glue has dried during the process of applying the enamel. To make sure that the enamel adheres, the glue is moistened by spraying it with distilled water from a distance of about 6 in (15 cm).

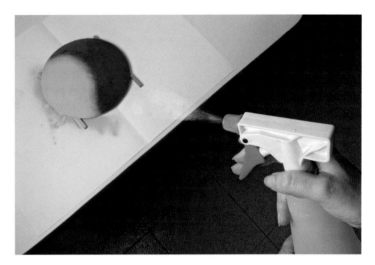

► 7. The piece is rotated by placing a spatula underneath while holding the dish from above with the other hand. It is held very carefully at the edges without touching the enamel too much, and then it is moved. The two colors are applied in a slight gradation, allowing the copper support to show through in the areas where the colors flow together.

▲ 8. The piece is placed in the kiln so that it will have minimal contact with the support. It is set on a metal stand shaped like a tripod that sits on the planche. The first firing is done at the normal working temperature.

◄ 9. It is removed from the kiln and allowed to cool, and the oxide is removed from the edges. Next, a second layer of enamels is added, overlaying and juxtaposing colors in some areas with gradations. The areas where the copper was allowed to show through are now covered with yellow.

▼ **10.** The piece is fired for the second time. Notice the gradations and juxtaposition of the colors, and the effect created by the transparent enamel over the oxidized copper.

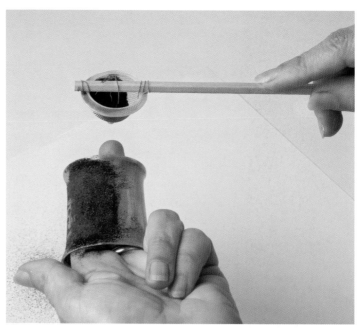

◄ **11.** Then the foot of the dessert stand is enameled. First it is annealed, and a coat of tragacanth gum is applied. The piece is held on the inside by hand or with tongs, and a layer of dark blue enamel is applied using the process described earlier. Then it is fired without counter enamel.

► **12.** The oxide is removed and the counter enamel and another layer of color are applied. It is fired a second time, and then it is enameled a third and last time. The ends of the piece are left without enamel because they will later be bonded to the bottom of the dish with glue. If they were enameled, the joint would be too wide and the proportions of the piece would be affected.

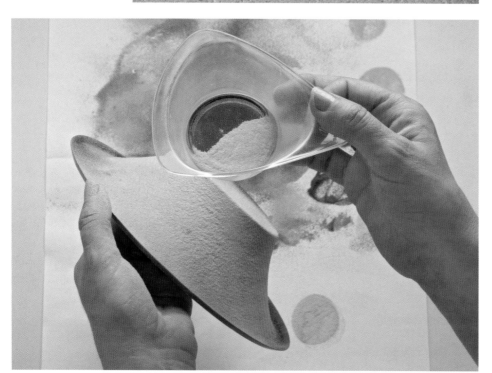

▲ **13.** Now work begins on the bowl. Glue is applied to the bottom exterior of the piece, and then it is enameled. To keep the glue completely damp so that the enamel will stick to it well, it is often sprayed with distilled water.

◄ **14.** The bowl is rotated as the enamel is applied, keeping its surface square to the sifter so that the enamel does not fall off.

◄ 15. When the back is finished, the piece is set on its base on the bed of extra enamel (when the stand is finished the base will not be visible). Glue is brushed on the vertical side of the interior, the enamels are applied, and sgraffito lines are made with a steel rod with a rounded tip.

▼ 16. The piece is then set on the firing stand used for the plate and fired for the first time.

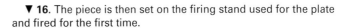

◄ 17. Next, a second layer of enamel is applied, glue is added, and the areas with oxidized copper (previously scratched) are covered with yellow enamel. The second firing is then done.

◄ 18. Some silver foil is applied to the front and back of the bowl and dish. A layer of tragacanth gum is brushed on the areas where the foil with be added; it is moved and arranged as desired, making some wrinkles to create effects, and adhered to the pieces.

▼ 19. Foils of different thickness were used, and overlaid in some areas.

◄ 20. In some areas, the foil is worked by scraping it with a wet carborundum stick.

◄ 21. Gold foil is also applied to the backs of the dish and bowl.

► 22. The cylindrical piece that is the foot of the dessert stand is also decorated with silver foil.

▲ 23. It is bonded with a brief firing, nearly half the time needed for normal enamels. The changes in the piece, along with the foil, are observed until it begins to acquire some color.

▲ 24. A second application of gold foil is applied to the piece that will be the bowl. Notice that the foil, both gold and silver, has been applied in a sequential pattern to emphasize the rhythm defined by the sgraffito lines.

► 25. Finally, the foil is bonded by firing in a kiln set somewhat lower than normal working temperature, around 1,560°F (850°C).

▲ **26.** Cobalt blue enamel is applied wet on certain areas of the silver foil, creating some faint gradations. They are left to dry, and the works are signed on the back with white vitreous paint. The bowl and the dessert stand go through the evaporation process and are then fired for the last time.

▲ **27.** Bases for the bowl and the dessert stand are custom made by a jeweler, as well as a rim for the dessert stand. The jeweler (in this case, F. Montells) makes the parts to order and fits them exactly to the enameled pieces. Then a coat of a special protective lacquer for metal is applied to the foil to protect it from scratching, and allowed to dry. Finally, the base is bonded to the enameled pieces with two-part adhesive.

◄ ▼ **28.** Here is the finished centerpiece and dessert stand set.

Panel (1)

*I*n this step-by-step example, Andreu Vilasís demonstrates the process for creating an enameled panel. In this project he uses flux, transparent enamels, and, for the central motif, opal grisaille. He employs vitreous paints to define and add color to very specific areas, in addition to silver and gold foils and liquid gold for certain details. Opal grisaille, also known as new grisaille, is the result of research conducted by the artist himself to update the technique for current materials; this grisaille produces similar results to the traditional grisaille using Limoges white. Andreu Vilasís is a specialist in this technique, which has become a hallmark of his work. This step-by-step is a clear example of the artist's expertise in the art of enameling, showcasing skills that he has developed throughout his long professional and academic career. We see his command of various techniques masterfully combined in this piece, where precision and perfection in execution are the outstanding features.

◄ 1. First, the design is sketched on paper. The dimensions of the sheet of copper are established, beginning with a panel 0.028 in (0.7 mm) thick.

► 2. Then, notes for the colors of the piece are made. To establish the mauve color of the composition's background, he uses different palettes as guides.

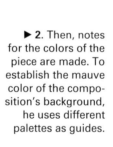

◄ 3. The sheet is cut out according to the dimensions of the project, 7 × 7 in (18 × 18 cm). It is measured and marked with the metal scribe according to the desired measurements and is later cut with the shears.

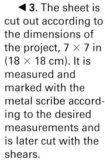

► 4. The sheet of metal is placed on the block and hammered using different hammers to create a slight curvature, somewhat more pronounced on the sides and the corners. The metal is cleaned.

▲ **5.** The sheet is placed on the worktable, which has been covered with a large sheet of paper, on two sticks with the reverse side facing up, and a layer of methylcellulose glue is applied.

▲ **6.** Then, the counter enamel is applied with the sifter from a distance of about 4 to 6 in (10–15 cm) above the piece.

◄ **7.** The resulting layer is perfectly even and homogenous. Distilled water is applied with a spray bottle from a reasonable distance to activate the glue and the adhesion of the enamel backing.

► **8.** Then, the piece is placed on the worktable, faceup on the two sticks, and a stencil cut in the shape of an oval measuring 4½ × 6¼ in (11.5 × 16 cm) is centered over it following the design of the sketch. It is secured with a few weights to make sure that it stays completely flat. An even layer of flux for copper is applied.

► **9.** The stencil is lifted very carefully and the edge is defined with a dry brush while removing the traces of flux.

◄ 10. The piece is fired for the first time. The firing time is shorter than normal to avoid the appearance of excessive oxidation in the area that was left exposed, which was protected by the previous reserve. It appears oxidized with a layer of calamina.

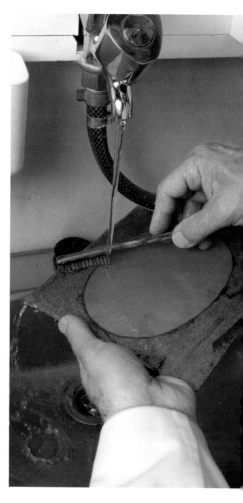

► 11. Before continuing, it is necessary to eliminate the remaining calamina; it comes off on its own by simply scrubbing with a brush under running water, and the piece is dried afterward. Notice that oxidation stains are left on purpose in subsequent phases to create textures.

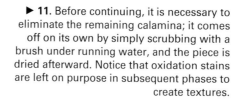

◄ 12. The piece is put back on the worktable with the two sticks, and a thin layer of flux is applied.

◄ 13. A second firing is done. In the picture, we can see the difference between the two areas, with different reddish tones under the briefly fired flux. Next, the oxidation from the edges of the piece is removed under running water with the carborundum stick.

► 14. Now the general forms are copied onto the piece. For this step, the outlines were transferred from the original design onto tracing paper.

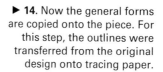

◀ **15.** Using white tracing paper the outlines are traced over with a round metal tip.

▶ **16.** The motif is transferred to the piece with carbon paper and then it is fired to fix the design (see page 79).

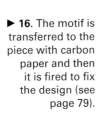

▶ **17.** Since the firing process is short and does not reach the optimum temperature for the flux to affect it, changes in the copper's oxidation are now very visible under the layer of flux; this phenomenon can be repeated in later firing phases. Transparent yellow enamel is applied wet with a brush over the figure's hair. This will turn into a warm tone once the grisaille is applied, and will contrast with the face.

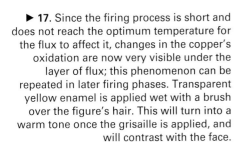

◀ **18.** The piece is fired for the fourth time for a normal period of time.

▶ **19.** Calamina is eliminated from the edges of the piece by rubbing with a bar of carborundum under running water, from the back side of the piece to the front. This will prevent calamina particles from depositing on the next layer of enamel and producing ugly, black stains.

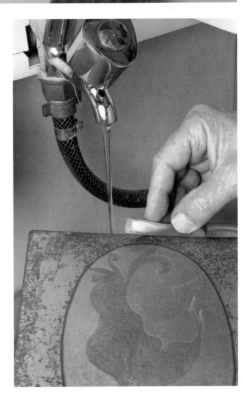

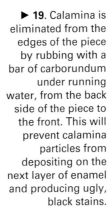

▲ **20.** To prepare to apply the gold foil, which will represent the element that holds the figure's hair, the outline of the form is traced on tracing paper.

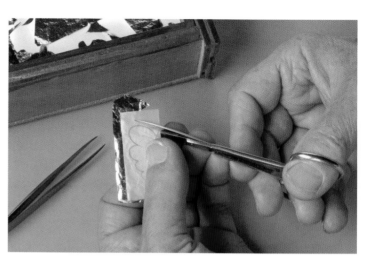

▲ **21.** The foil shape, which was prepared before (see page 80), is cut out with very sharp sewing scissors.

▲ **22.** To make sure that the gold foil fits perfectly on the design, it is laid very carefully over the original drawing with the help of tweezers.

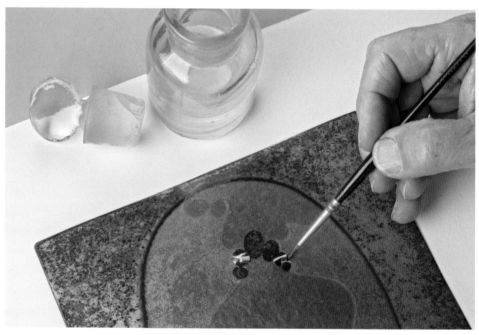

▲ **23.** Tragacanth glue is applied over the area designated for the foil. Then, the foil is picked up with the brush and placed according to the original design, passing the brush over the surface until the piece is completely flat. After that, the remaining forms of the design are drawn with vitreous paint, which will serve as a guide for the grisaille.

◄ **24.** The foil and the vitreous paint are fixed by firing.

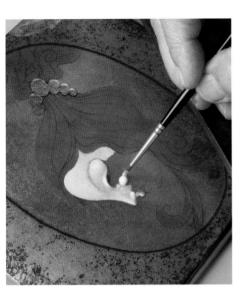

◄ 25. The figure's face and the hair are created with the new grisaille technique, using white opalescent enamel. It is applied with the brush over the face, following the forms of the design, depositing more material in the areas that are to appear lighter. We continue modeling to create chiaroscuro effects.

▲ 26. The enamel is distributed using the steel point, outlining the oval of the face as well as the eye, nose, and mouth. Soft gradations are created in the chest area, leaving the area below the face darker. We continue applying enamel on the head, modeling the strands of hair. Finally, green transparent enamel is applied in the center of each of the foil ovals to create the effect of a gem.

◄ 27. The piece is fired a sixth time and the calamina is eliminated from the edges of the support. Next, a second layer of grisaille is applied.

► 28. The forms of the face and the hair are modeled, creating a bas-relief with the enamel. The work should progress in an orderly fashion, first the face and then the hair, strand by strand.

▲ 29. The piece is fired for the seventh time. The figure's face and chest are in slight contrast with the hair, which has a warmer tone thanks to the subtle yellow enamel below, which shows through the transparent grisaille. The oxidation is removed from the edges.

◀ 30. Then, the area surrounding the oval is covered with transparent mauve enamel, which is applied with the sifter, even on the three hair strands made of grisaille that extend beyond the borders of the oval. Next, using a bridge so as not to touch the mauve area still to be fired, a third layer of enamel over the face and chest is applied, modeling the forms.

▶ 31. The enamel is fired one last time. The hair strands become transparent under the layer of mauve enamel and appear in a slightly darker tone.

▼ 32. To finish modeling the face, the hair strands are defined, the lips are painted, and shadows are added with vitreous paints. Also, some of the upper strands of hair are extended and defined, creating a soft gradation with paint. The piece is fired.

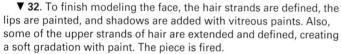

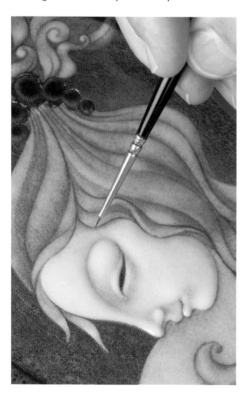

▲ 33. The piece is finished with a wavy border of liquid silver. A few circular details are also added to the brooch on the hair with liquid gold.

◄ 34. To prepare the silver, it is kneaded with paraffin. Then it is applied with the brush, creating a wavy border around the oval, and the artist signs the piece. Next, details are added with the liquid gold, which has also been kneaded with paraffin. Once finished it is left to evaporate following the same process as vitreous paints (see pages 94–95). At the time of application the silver is shiny, but it turns dark gray, almost toasted, during this process. This firing is critical. It should be very gentle and brief, faster than with vitreous paint. The piece does not turn glossy, so it has to be monitored until the color becomes somewhat whiter, at which time it will be taken out. The result is a very light, matte gray color, similar to the way the enamel looks in powder form.

► 35. The silver and the gold are polished with an agate tip (or with a rounded steel tip), rubbing until they take on a characteristic metallic shine. Firing is an extremely important step; if after rubbing with the agate the silver comes off, it means that the firing time was insufficient. On the other hand, firing it too long would make the metal matte, which would be impossible to polish.

► 36. The work completely finished.

139

Panel (2)

*I*n this step-by-step, Montserrat Mainar shows us how to create a panel entitled Il bianco e dolce cigno (The White and Gentle Swan), *inspired by the famous madrigal by Flemish composer Jaques Arcadelt (1505–1567). It is made on a flat sheet of copper 0.020 in (0.5 mm) thick with the edges bent at a right angle, which makes the support stronger and harder to warp. The enamel is applied dry, the reserves are made with stencils, and the details, shading, and areas of color are finished with vitreous paint. The patterns are cut out following the shapes and colors of the original design. They are layered to create the forms of the design with dry enamel. The artist has explored the possibilities of this technique for many years, using it throughout her professional career in the execution of countless pieces.*

◄ **1.** First, the general forms of the piece are sketched. Then, the design is reproduced in color at actual size (the support measures 6¼ × 10⅝ in [16 × 27 cm]).

▲ **2.** The different patterns are made using the full-scale design as a guide, tracing the shapes onto tissue paper. Then they are copied using tracing paper to make the stencils, which are cut out with a utility knife.

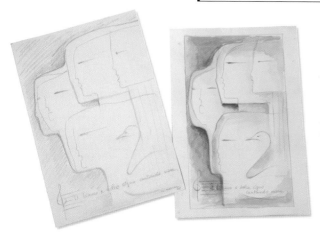

◄ **3.** Four stencils will be used, which are shown in order from left to right. The edges of the support have been drawn on all of them, and small notches have been cut out in all four corners, which will help in fitting the pattern perfectly onto the support. Also, each of them has been labeled with the order, firing phase, and number or code of the enamel that will be used. The first two (on the left side of the photo) will be used for the background, the third one (top right) will be used to apply the blue areas, and the last one (bottom right) will help create the forms.

▶ ▶ **4.** First, the counter enamel is applied on the back side of the support, and it is fired. Then the top surface of the copper is cleaned. No flux is applied over the copper; instead, the enamels are applied directly. The sheet of copper will not be affected whatsoever when the counter enamel is fired thanks to the shape of the sheet and the bent corners.

▲ **5.** The support is placed on the work-table over a clean sheet of paper, and the stencil is centered on it, guided by the notches. Using a sifter, we apply an even layer of lilac transparent enamel over the area that is not covered by the reserve.

▲ **6.** We lift the stencil very carefully, grabbing the upper corner and the opposite lower corner to prevent the enamel from smearing. An area of lilac color will have formed, which matches the one in the original design.

▲ **7.** Then, we proceed with the rest of the background. With the second pattern we cover the previously enameled area; after centering it perfectly, we apply white opaque enamel on the exposed area. The enamel is not applied evenly because we want to create gradations.

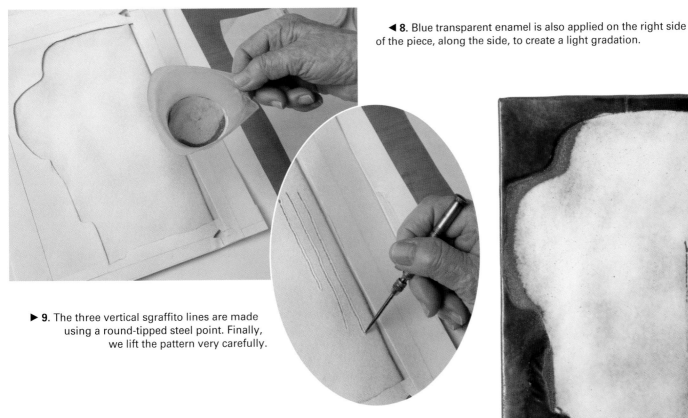

◀ **8.** Blue transparent enamel is also applied on the right side of the piece, along the side, to create a light gradation.

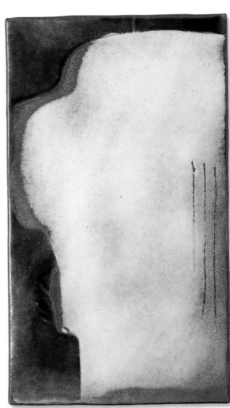

▶ **9.** The three vertical sgraffito lines are made using a round-tipped steel point. Finally, we lift the pattern very carefully.

▶ **10.** The piece is fired for the first time. The firing will be stronger than usual, to achieve the effects caused by oxidation of the support. This firing will also provide the green tones that result from firing the enamel with copper oxide, which are especially visible on the white. This is a view of the piece after it has cooled off.

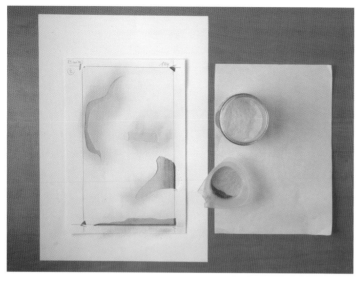

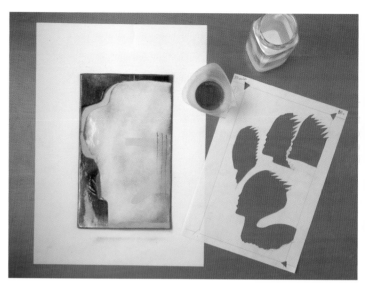

▲ **11.** Then, the enamels are applied, before being fired for the second and last time. The third stencil is placed on the piece, and blue transparent enamel is applied, focusing on the central form, where an even layer is applied. Less enamel is used for the form on the left, and a light gradation is used for the lower and right shapes.

▲ **12.** At this point, the fourth stencil is used to make the other shapes by applying a second layer of white opaque enamel.

▶ **13.** Here, the enamel has also been applied with various gradations; more enamel has been used on the left side and less on the right.

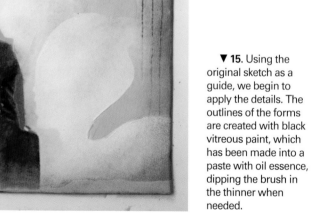

◀ **14.** New lilac and green transparent enamels are sprinkled over the previously fired layer to achieve a deeper color, as shown in the sketch. The piece is fired for the second time.

▼ **15.** Using the original sketch as a guide, we begin to apply the details. The outlines of the forms are created with black vitreous paint, which has been made into a paste with oil essence, dipping the brush in the thinner when needed.

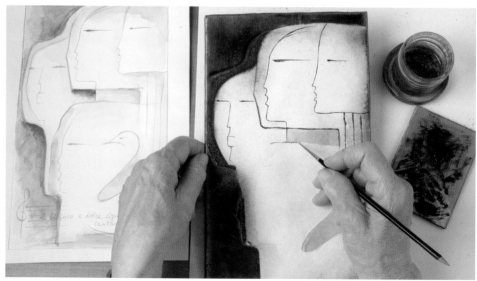

▶ **16.** We proceed in an orderly fashion, working by area. When the forms have been defined with the black paint, the areas of color are applied with vitreous paint, using gradations where needed.

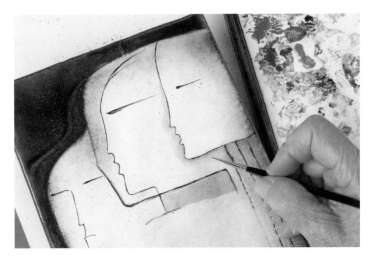

▼ **17.** The rest of the forms are outlined and shadows added. The wing of the swan is also drawn, as well as the treble clef with the first words of the madrigal. This is followed by the application of blue enamel on the left side of the composition, which was left uncovered. The vitreous paints are left to evaporate, and the piece is fired for the third time.

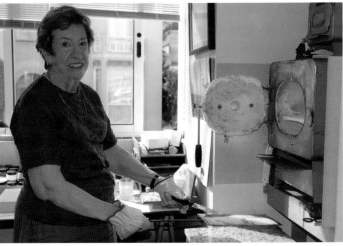

▲ **18.** The final touches are added, and the artist signs the piece with vitreous paint. The last evaporation and firing of the piece take place.

▶ **19.** The finished work.

Pendant

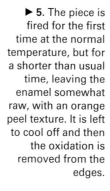

*I*n this exercise we demonstrate how to make a pendant, Ovals. It is an original piece by Gemma Moles, executed with the stained-glass technique. The artist, in a display of technical mastery, makes a large stained-glass object in a single piece using a thin copper support. It is constructed in phases on a temporary mica base: First, the flux is applied and the piece is fired, and then a blue layer of transparent enamel is applied and fired. She proceeds in this fashion to ensure the proper adhesion of the stained glass to the support and to achieve the desired thickness; this will make the enamel more durable and maintain the transparency of the stained glass. Finally, it is decorated with vitreous paint.

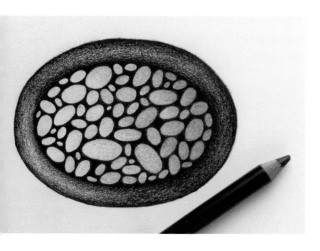

◀ 1. First, a pencil sketch of the piece is made on paper. The piece consists of an outer copper ring enameled in black and a large blue stained-glass center with oval shapes made with vitreous paint.

▶ 2. The pattern of the copper ring is drawn with a pencil on contact paper and adhered to the metal sheet (0.031 in [0.8 mm]). We make a small hole in it with the electric drill through which we will pass the saw blade. We attach the blade to the saw. Then, the piece is cut out following the pattern.

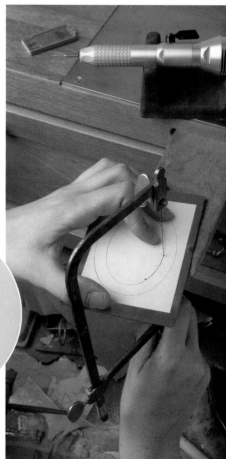

▶ 3. The outer measurements of the copper piece are 2¼ × 3 inches (5.8 × 7.8 cm) with an interior opening of 1½ × 2⅜ inches (4 × 6 cm) (where the stained glass will be located) and ¾ in (1.8 cm) wide.

◀ 4. Counter enamel and a layer of black opaque enamel will be applied wet to the front of the piece with a brush.

▶ 5. The piece is fired for the first time at the normal temperature, but for a shorter than usual time, leaving the enamel somewhat raw, with an orange peel texture. It is left to cool off and then the oxidation is removed from the edges.

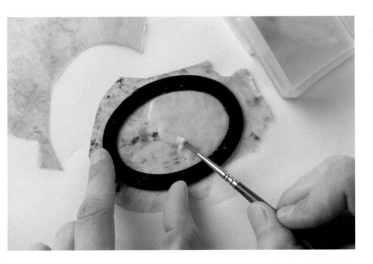

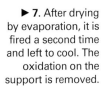

◄ 6. The piece is placed on a temporary mica base, a little bit larger than the piece itself, that has already been prepared (see page 117). A very thin layer of flux is applied, mixed in suspension with distilled water to the consistency of a paste. The flux adheres to the support and becomes the base of the stained glass.

► 7. After drying by evaporation, it is fired a second time and left to cool. The oxidation on the support is removed.

◄ 8. At this time, the second layer of blue transparent enamel is applied with a brush until a thin, even layer is achieved. The colorless base (flux) guarantees the transparency of the stained glass; the application of two layers of blue enamel will make the piece look darker and less transparent.

▲ 9. The piece is fired for the third time, and the mica is removed by rubbing with a hard-bristle brush under running water; the oxidation from the edges is also removed. Using the sketch as a guide, the artist draws the ovals inside of the stained glass with black vitreous paint. At this point, we add a layer of opaque black enamel over the ring. Finally, the appropriate evaporation and firing (directly on the planche) for the vitreous paint takes place. The texture of the ring's black enamel resembles a frosted surface.

► 10. The finished pendant with braces and a silver chain.

Sculpture

*I*n this last step-by-step, Rafael Arroyo demonstrates the process for creating his original sculpture Azulenca. This piece is an excellent example of the artist's work, combining a sculptural figure, made with assembled pieces, with enamel creations made with a variety of techniques and resources. This is also a magnificent example of the many possibilities that enameling offers for three-dimensional and rounded pieces. Starting with a 0.016-in thick (0.4 mm) copper sheet, the artist has used transparent and opalescent enamels to achieve chromatic and tonal gradations, combining various techniques: foils, cloisonné, bas-relief enameling, and stained-glass details. This very involved process results in a unique piece that showcases both the artist's personality and his technical mastery of enameling.

▼ **1.** First, a design is created for the project. Several drawings are made of different perspectives of the piece, keeping in mind that the forms must later fit into the three-dimensional sculpture. The design is sketched in color as well, and the enamels and techniques that will be employed are listed.

▼ **2.** Using the sketch as a guide, the artist begins constructing the three-dimensional model. For this, he uses heavy paper because it is tough yet bendable, similar to the sheet of metal that will be used to make the piece.

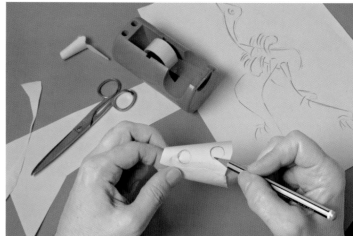

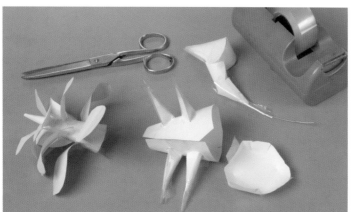

▲ **3.** Actual-size prototypes of all the pieces that will form the sculpture are cut out and put together with tape. Wire is added where needed (in the neck) to make sure they are properly secured.

► **4.** The three-dimensional prototype is finished, measuring 16 in (40 cm) tall. It is very important that the parts fit together perfectly, because the paper pieces will be used as patterns to create the sculpture.

▶ **24.** Gold foil is applied on the pieces that form the neck, legs, and body of the sculpture, and also on the back and front sides of the feathers; then, silver foil is applied on the head. The foils enrich the surfaces and add movement to the composition. They are fixed by firing them.

▼ **25.** The pieces for the body and legs are held with tweezers, and a layer of transparent yellow gold enamel is applied wet.

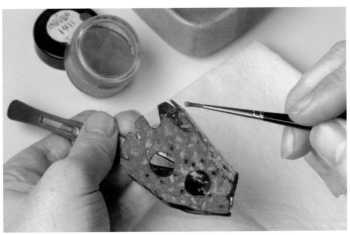

▶ **26.** The enameling of the large pieces is done in two steps; first, enamel is applied on the upper part and fired, and then the lower part is done and the piece is fired again. Both times, the enamel is dried under a strong light because it should be completely dry before it is fired.

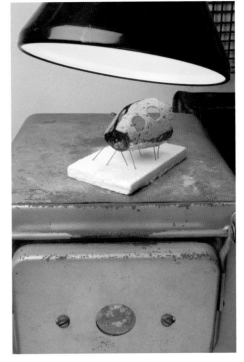

▲ **27.** Using your color and foil tests as a reference, the cloisonné enamels are applied on the head, neck, and wings. A layer of wet, white opal enamel is applied on the head of the sculpture before it is fired and cleaned. Then, transparent blue and green enamels are applied.

▶ **28.** The cloisonné of the feathers are wet packed with opaque enamels inside, and transparent yellow gold enamel, similar to the one used on the other parts of the sculpture, is applied to the base.

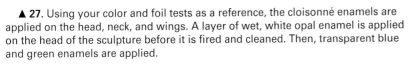

◄ 29. The sculpture has some details made with the plique-à-jour technique on the head and the lower part of the body. They are done using round copper wire 0.024 in (0.6 mm) in diameter, which will be bent on one end to form a small circle. Enamel is applied, a bit more granular than usual.

▼ 30. The pieces are fired for the first time, during which it is important to monitor the enamels to make sure that they vitrify. When they acquire a grainy consistency, they are pulled out of the kiln.

▼ 31. We begin to assemble the piece. To put the parts together we use the colored marks (step 19) as a reference, attaching them with 0.016-in diameter (0.4 mm) copper wire. The legs are made with round wire that is 0.050-in (1.3 mm) thick. To hold the piece in place on the pedestal, we make several holes with a drill and the appropriate bit, inserting the wire to make an invisible holder.

▲ 32. We also assemble the neck with the feathers and the head, using 0.050-in (1.3 mm) wire as backing. Then the stained-glass pieces (hair) are assembled by inserting their lower ends into the holes of the head; they are adjusted with pliers.

▲ 33. The two main parts of the sculpture are assembled the same way. The joints should not be forced as this can cause tension, which could compromise the integrity of the enamel.

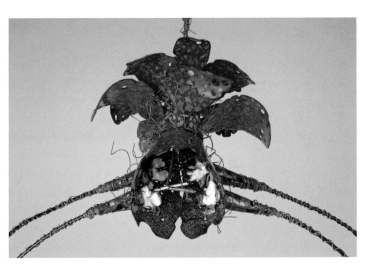

▲ **34.** The insides of the legs are filled with expanded polystyrene to counteract the tension produced by the weight of the pieces they support. This is done because the enamel, although strong, is a very delicate material and could come off as a result of any warping or tension in the pieces.

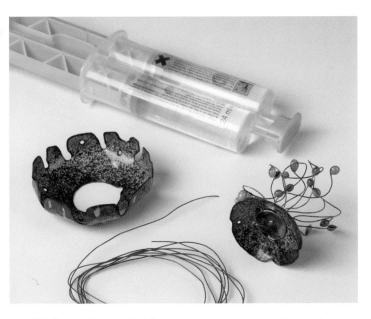

▲ **35.** To attach the tail of the sculpture, a two-part adhesive is used instead of wires, which would be too complicated.

▶ **36.** The finished work.

▶ Meritxell Castellano (Sabadell, Spain). Pendants, 2006–2007. Silver alloy. Champlevé and bas-relief (etched with acid and enameled with transparent enamels). Various sizes, between 1⅜ and 2 in (3.5 and 5 cm) in diameter.

◀ Núria L. Ribalta (Barcelona, Spain). *Nosaltres* (left) and *Meteorit* (right), brooches from the series "The Colors of Barcelona," 1998. Enamel painted over copper, metalwork by Imma Gibert and Tomàs Palos, respectively. 2½ × 2⅝ and 2 × 3⅜ in (6.2 × 6.5 and 5 × 8.5 cm).

▶ Dominique Gilbert (Le Vigen, France). *Naisance du signe*, 2007. Champlevé and cloisonné over gilded copper. 8½ × 4¾ in (21 × 12 cm).

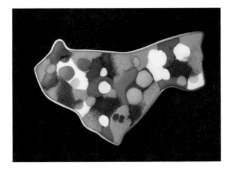

▶ B. Zubizarreta (Barcelona, Spain). *Puppy*, 2008. Enamel painted with opaque colors over silver. 2 × 2³⁄₁₆ in (5 × 5.5 cm).

▲ Núria L. Ribalta (Barcelona, Spain). *CIDAE Trophy*, 2007. Enamel painted over copper with silver and gold foils. Metalwork by Francesc Montells in silver, with the neck of the cup etched. 7 × 2³⁄₄ × 2 in (18 × 7 × 5 cm). Trophy designed for the International Exposition "El Món de L'esmalt" (Tarragona, Spain).

▲ Montserrat Mainar (Barcelona, Spain). *Mythological Athlete*, 1997. Enamel painted with mixed technique (transparencies, opalescent enamel, and glass) over copper. 11³⁄₄ × 15³⁄₄ in (30 × 40 cm).

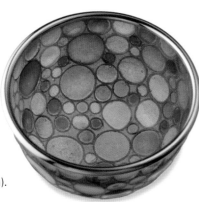

▶ Gemma Moles (Barcelona, Spain). *Circles*, 2000. Three-dimensional stained-glass bowl made with silver wire and transparent enamel. 1³⁄₈ × 2³⁄₄ in (3.5 × 7 cm).

▶ Andreu Vilasís (Barcelona, Spain). *Guitar*, 2007. Painted enamel and foils over copper, dyed wood. 10 × 10 in (25 × 25 cm). This piece was awarded the "Gran Premio Internacional" at the 2007 Biennial of Enamel Art in Vilnius, Lithuania.

▼ Jessica Meroño (Barcelona, Spain). *París*, 2007. Ring, earrings, and pendant painted adornment over enamel. Ring: ¾ × ¾ × 2 in (1.8 × 1.8 × 2.5 cm); earrings: ½ × ½ in (1.2 × 1.2 cm); pendant: ⅝ × ⅝ × ¼ in (1.7 × 1.7 × 0.7 cm).

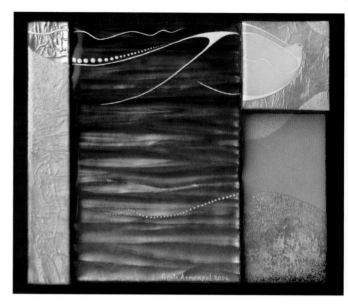

▲ Perote Armengol (Barcelona, Spain). *Color Transformation*, 2004. Enamel painted over textured copper and foils. 4 × 3.5 in (10.2 × 9 cm).

◄ Núria L. Ribalta (Barcelona, Spain). *Surrealist Gaze II*, 1986. Miniature over copper mounted in eyeglasses. 6 × 2 in (15.5 × 5 cm).

◄ Rafael Arroyo (Barcelona, Spain). *Personaje Galliforme*, 2004. Sculpture made of copper and fired enamel with mixed techniques. 9 × 13¾ × 4 in (23 × 35 × 20 cm).

▲ Bagués-Masriera Jewelers (Barcelona, Spain). Bracelet from the collection "Spring Concert," 2008. Eighteen-karat white and yellow gold with fired enamel and brilliant-cut diamonds (reference BPO-60). 8¾ × 1¾ in (223 × 45.94 mm).

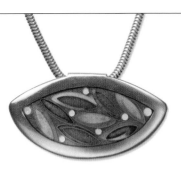

▶ Carolyn Delzoppo (Mullumbimby, Australia). *Pendant*, 1998. Silver cloisonné over silver with shiny finish. 1 × 1⅞ in (2.5 × 4.7 cm).

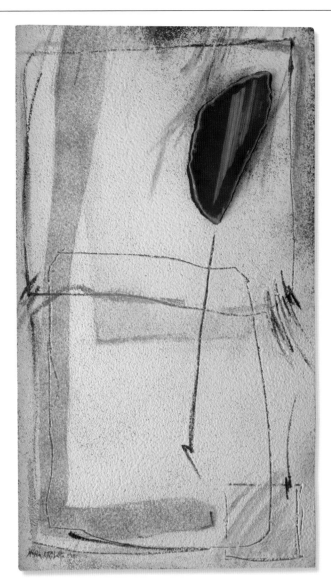

◀ Edmund Massow (Geisenfeld, Germany). *Brooch*, 2003. Silver cloisonné over silver with satin finish. 1¾ × 1¾ in (4.5 × 4.5 cm).

▲ Núria L. Ribalta (Barcelona, Spain), *El mite de Danae*, from the series "Erotic Suite," 1990. Enamel painted over copper with sgraffito and enameled pencil and wax. 10⅝ × 6 in (27 × 15 cm).

▲ Kioko Iio (Tokyo, Japan). *Metod of Live Out*, 1995. Cloisonné over copper. 12¼ × 12¼ × 12¼ in (31 × 31 × 31 cm).

▶ Núria L. Ribalta (Barcelona, Spain). *Ornegre 1*, 2004. Bowl with a pedestal, painted and sgraffito enamel with gold foil over copper and aluminum rim. 4 × 12 in diameter (10 × 30 cm).

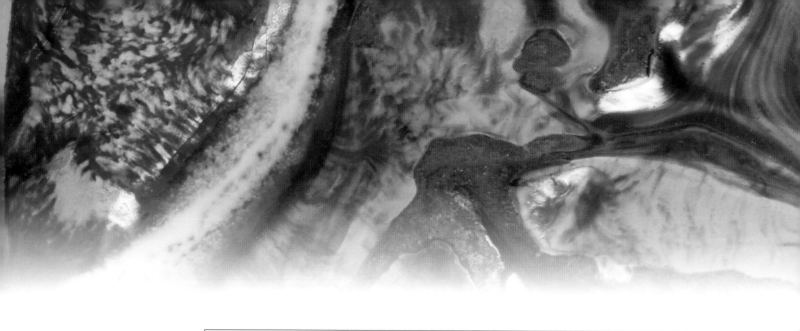

Glossary

a

Annealing. Very gently heating metal in a kiln or with a torch until it begins to glow or turn cherry red. After cooling, it will have a layer of calamine. This is done to degrease and restore flexibility to metal that has been hammered, rolled, or work hardened, and to facilitate the pickling process.

b

Bas-relief. A technique that consists of engraving or chiseling metal to make a pattern or design, which creates a chiaroscuro effect when it is filled with transparent enamel. The difference in light intensity creates the chiaroscuro effect of the piece.

Basse-taille. Bas-relief.

Burnishing. Polishing metal by rubbing it with an agate or steel tool with a round tip.

c

Champlevé. A technique based on filling hollowed areas of a metal support with enamel. The hollows are made in the metal with cutting tools or chemical etching (acid). This results in a piece with a smooth surface with alternating enamel and metal.

Chasing. A metalworking technique consisting of modeling metal with punches, tapping them to create incised designs.

Cloisonné. A technique that involves filling wire cells with enamel. The cells are created by fusing metal wire to a support, which separates the areas of enamel. The cells are arranged in the shape of the design and fused to a layer of enamel or soldered directly to the metal.

Copper Oxide. Also known as cupric oxide or calamina, the layer that forms on the surface of copper when it is oxidized by heat.

Corrosion. The decomposition of metal caused by the action of an acid that provokes a chemical oxygen reduction reaction, destroying areas of the metal that are not protected. In the art of enamel, the metal supports of the pieces can be hollowed by corrosion for cloisonné and bas-relief work.

Counter Enamel. A layer or layers of enamel applied to the back of the piece. This counters the expansion and contraction of the metal, keeps the support from oxidizing, and prevents cracking and chipping.

e

Émail Peint. Painted enamel.

Enamel Relief. Also known as ronde bosse, enamel applied to pieces that are generally small and three-dimensional, with high-relief repoussé or embossing work. These can be solid or hollow pieces.

Essences. Oily liquid substances made by mixing hydrocarbons extracted from different kinds of plants, which have characteristics similar to oils but are very volatile. They are used as agglutinates for vitreous paint, for liquid gold and silver, and also for Limoges white.

Evaporation. The process by which the agglutinate in Limoges white and vitreous paint disappears, done by putting pieces in the kiln. It also refers to drying enamel that is applied wet before the pieces are fired.